A

SURGEON'S

WAR

My Year in Vietnam

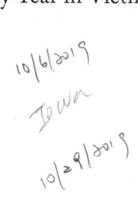

CONTENTS

THE STORY BEHIND THE COVER PHOTO

In April 1966, Marine Lance Corporal Perry Shinneman sustained life-threatening wounds in Vietnam. He was treated by the author and his medical team, as detailed in Chapter XXII of this book: "Saving Lance Corporal Shinneman." The author wondered, as he always did, if his patient made it home. This photo of Corporal Shinneman returning to the United States, and to his wife, Shirley, was taken by Ray Mews for the *Argus Leader* newspaper of Sioux Falls, South Dakota. Astor & Lenox wishes to thank Shaleen Langenfeld, Perry and Shirley's daughter, of Sioux Falls, and Maricarroll Kueter, executive editor of the *Argus Leader*, both of whom kindly granted permission to use the image.

ACKNOWLEDGMENTS

10/6/2019

I have written this book, above all other reasons, to honor the Marines who served in Vietnam, and their families, who surely suffered. I am grateful to the team of fellow doctors, corpsmen, and staff who were there with me, at C Med and the Navy hospital at Da Nang, in 1965 and 1966. My apologies to any colleagues who were present during the events described in this book, yet whose involvement I did not mention. There were dozens, if not hundreds, of Marines in Vietnam whose competence and teamwork made my story possible.

I also offer thanks to Jason Brown, a former Wallace Stegner Fellow at Stanford University, who read the first draft of this book and saw its promise. With his questions, he guided me and prodded me to delve into the story ever deeper. My path to remembering, the writing down of memories, and the healing that resulted, began in 1998, with a poetry-writing class I took at Stanford University, taught by Jennifer Richter, another Stegner Fellow. Through her example, our class learned how truly to listen to each other. We continue to meet monthly and support each other as writers. My thanks to Nancy Mohr, Mary Lee McNeal, Marian Slattery, Narada Hess, Nancy Etchemendy, Lisa Rosenberg, and especially to Rick Mamelok for his thoughtful review of this entire manuscript.

Over the past two years, I have also been privileged to be

a part of Pegasus Physicians, a group of doctors writing about their experiences in the field of medicine, which is supported by the Arts, Humanities and Medicine Program at Stanford School of Medicine. We are led by Hans Steiner, Audrey Shafer, and Irvin D. Yalom. Others in the group are Randall Weingarten, Richard Shaw, Jim Lock, John Van Natta, Lauren Pischel, Shaili Jain, and Bill Meffert.

Finally I am grateful to Terence Clarke and Ivory Madison, Director of Publishing and CEO/Publisher, respectively, at Astor & Lenox, who worked patiently and generously with me, over the course of two years, to make the final telling possible.

FOREWORD

10|6|20 19

The Vietnamese people have been fighting for their independence for a millennium, against the Chinese, then the French, the Japanese, the French once more, and finally against each other and, in the cases of the North Vietnamese and the Viet Cong, against the Americans. As we came to learn, the Vietnamese are warriors.

In the modern era, France occupied all of Indochina in the nineteenth century, as part of their colonial empire. During World War II, the Japanese stationed troops in Vietnam, in an agreement with the French Vichy Government. As soon as the war ended in 1945, Ho Chi Minh declared Vietnam's independence, thus beginning the second French phase of their struggle.

In that classic asymmetrical war waged by a weaker power against a much stronger one—ominously foreshadowing the United States' experience—the communists engaged in a battle of attrition, ultimately exhausting the more powerful French army. They finally defeated the French at the famous (or infamous) battle of Dien Bien Phu, in 1954. The United States partially financed the French in that war and provided some of the weaponry. The French pleaded for direct U.S. airstrikes around Dien Bien Phu, but President Eisenhower refused, fearing accusations of American colonialism.

At an international convention in Geneva in 1954, the decision was taken to divide the country at the 17th parallel, with a communist north, and a nationalist south. An all-country election was to be held in 1956, which never took place. The U.S. refused to sign the agreement, fearing that Ho Chi Minh would win in a landslide.

From the takeover of China by the communists in 1949, the U.S. feared a loss of all of South East Asia, beginning with South Vietnam. This was the so-called "Domino Theory." By 1965, the South Vietnamese were indeed close to collapse, prompting President Johnson to initiate the truly American phase of the Vietnam war by ordering elements of the 3rd Marine Division to land at Da Nang.

That decision dramatically changed world history, and in the process ensnared Ward Trueblood.

Henry Ward Trueblood grew up in a small town in Iowa in the 1940s and 50s, the son of a physician, in a family of Quakers. He accompanied his dad on rounds, and soon had no doubt that he, too, would become a physician. By 1965, he was midway through the training program at the Hospital of the University of Pennsylvania when his draft number for the U.S. Navy came up. His Quaker faith would have allowed him to obtain conscientious objector status. Instead he chose to enter the Navy as a physician. Moreover, refusing the safety of a clinic-type tour of duty, he volunteered for Vietnam.

This was a brave decision on Ward's part. Physicians in Vietnam were by no means safe from the action in the field. A colleague of mine, at that same time in the midst of his surgical training in Boston, made the same decision to volunteer for Vietnam, and was killed during the Tet Offensive of 1968.

In *A Surgeon's War*, we are with Ward Trueblood at C Med (similar to a Mobile Army Surgical Hospital, or MASH), and then at the Navy hospital near Da Nang. He takes us into his confidence as he faces danger, misery, suffering, mutilation, and death on a scale he could scarcely have imagined. We learn that he was acutely aware of his own shortcomings and his lack of senior resident experience, not to mention his to-that-moment minimal background in trauma training. Wisely, he learned from anyone who could help, including enlisted corpsmen as well as other fully trained surgeons at C Med. His maturation as a surgeon unfolds as he is involved with one patient with multiple, complex wounds after another. He assists his senior colleagues until he himself is ready to be the principal surgeon. He learns what works and what doesn't. He identifies his mistakes unflinchingly, and vows never to repeat them.

That mindset is what makes a great surgeon.

We learn how Ward deals with the deaths of young Marines. He tries to manage his grief while facing the enormity of the tragedy. His grief intensifies especially in those moments when he feels he may have committed a surgical error. Most of all, he faces the limits of what anyone can accomplish in what is essentially a hopeless setting. He sometimes learns that not intervening is the best choice for the patient.

Ward returned home after his tour of duty ended, resumed his surgical training, and subsequently launched what has become a successful surgical career at Stanford University. Decades later, haunted by his wartime experience, he wrote this memoir. He may have left Vietnam many years ago, but Vietnam never left him. I know quite well—because I served in Vietnam with Ward—that he made a vow after viewing body bags at C Med: "I want my life to be an act of gratitude for the very gift of life."

Ward Trueblood has done that, and I can't imagine a better outcome for him, or anyone else who served.

—Gerald Moss M.D.
Dean Emeritus
University of Illinois at Chicago, College of Medicine
Former Commander, United States Navy Reserve, 1965 to 1968
Officer in Charge, Frozen Blood Program, Da Nang, Vietnam

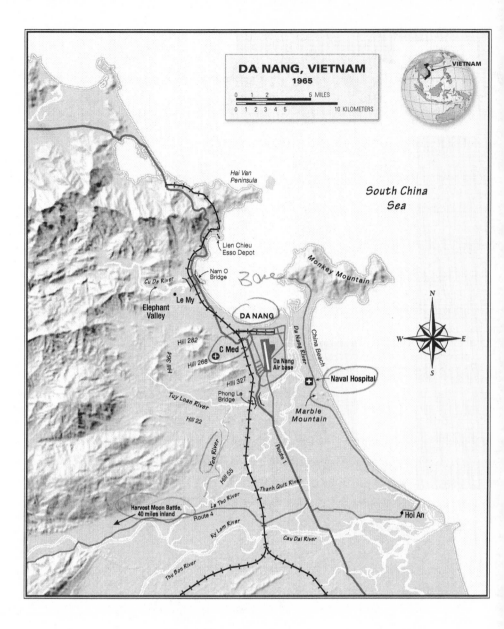

DA NANG, VIETNAM
1965

0   1   2   5 MILES

0 1 2 3 4 5   10 KILOMETERS

VIETNAM

South China
Sea

Hai Van
Peninsula

Lien Chieu
Esso Depot

Nam O
Bridge

Cu De River

Elephant
Valley

Le My

Monkey Mountain

DA NANG

Hill 282

C Med

Hill 364

Hill 268

Hill 327

Da Nang
Air base

Da Nang River

China Beach

N

W   E

S

Naval Hospital

Tuy Loan River

Phong Le
Bridge

Marble
Mountain

Hill 22

Yen River

Hill 55

Route 1

Harvest Moon Battle,
40 miles inland

La Tho River

Route 4

Thanh Quit River

Hoi An

Ky Lam River

Cau Dai River

Thu Bon River

PREFACE

There is a general ignorance about the true cost of war. I know this ignorance first hand, thinking of the gap between what I thought I knew the day I received my draft notice in July 1965, and now, as I write about what it was like to be both the treating doctor and the witness to human sacrifice.

My telling has been delayed. What happened in that year in Da Nang initially became locked in my mind behind a self-protective shield. After my return from Vietnam, I hurried into a life that didn't include anything from that experience: wedding plans, finishing my surgical training, having a family, and building a surgical career. Early on, the war experience was just too big for me to handle.

Finally, after years of dealing with sporadic episodes of unexplained anger and weeping, and frequent, recurring nightmares of operating on wounds too big to manage, I began reading my letters home from Vietnam, and then writing this memoir.

I wanted to write about one man's journey from a sheltered life into the madness of war. So many lives and families were ruined by the war, for decades after. It is a cycle that appears to repeat every generation, as it did for my father and then for me. Yet as a society, each younger generation of soldiers, families, and politicians have still somehow not learned the true cost of war, until they go through it themselves.

I was able to survive the shattering of my pre-Vietnam worldview and to find a new way to see a world that was just as moral while being more rooted in reality. I was one of the lucky ones who got out alive and whole. But the true cost of war, paid by others, never left me. Indeed it left a shadow over my soul.

—H. Ward Trueblood

CHAPTER I

Operation Harvest Moon, I Corps, Vietnam, December 1965

Rain was falling at C Med. All of us had been up working most of the night. I had been part of this team, of thirteen doctors, for three months now. As I ate breakfast with the operating room (OR) corpsmen, we complained about the CBS News television crew and *Time* magazine photographer who'd been getting in our way for the last twenty-four hours. Suddenly, our commander, Dr. Richard Escajeda, appeared in the doorway. A brusque personality, Escajeda had been among the medical personnel to come ashore with the first large contingent of Marines, at Chu Lai, earlier in the year. On this occasion, he seemed very serious—which was not his usual cavalier demeanor. I wasn't the only one jolted by this, although I was the only one he addressed. "Trueblood, get your bed roll, flak jacket, and helmet. I'm sending you to replace Waldron at Harvest Moon. The helicopter will be here in ten minutes."

This order from Escajeda left me worried about Dr. Lloyd Waldron, my tent-mate and best friend for the last three months. I was searching for words while Escajeda chewed on his cigar. He seemed to be thinking about something else. By the time I found my voice, he was marching away from the tent. I left my powdered eggs half-eaten and caught him on his way to his next command decision.

"Is Waldron okay?" I asked, trying not to let on I was scared.

Escajeda stopped walking and looked into my eyes. He even took the cigar out of his mouth, which he didn't usually do.

"Yes, Ward-o. We just need Waldron here more than we need you. Tell him to brief you when you get there." Escajeda walked off.

Harvest Moon had nothing to do with autumn, as it had back home. Harvest Moon was the name of a major coordinated attack by the 3rd Battalion, 3rd Marines, and 2nd Battalion, 7th Marines, along with parts of the Army of the Republic of Vietnam (ARVN), against the 1st Viet Cong Regiment, near the Laotian border of I Corps. It would eventually result in forty-five Marines killed and two-hundred eighteen wounded. Waldron was part of a "shock team," as it was called, sent to the battle staging area to be closer to the wounded.

I wasn't sure that Escajeda, whom I liked and respected, always took our welfare fully into account when he made these quick decisions. In fact, I was sure he didn't. Less than a month earlier, in November, in response to an emergency call for a doctor in the jungle, he'd sent me on a flight at nighttime. After we had reached the distressed unit by helicopter and found landing in the forested terrain impossible, I had been asked to rappel blindly into the area, to treat the wounded man. I declined, and was sure at the time that I would be reprimanded for refusing an order. I was sure I'd be chastised as a coward as well.

But when I made it back to C Med, Escajeda complimented me on my "good thinking." It turned out that the Marine had not actually been wounded, but was delirious from cerebral malaria. There was nothing I could have done for him at night in the jungle. We later learned that the call we had received had not even followed the usual chain of command, which would have included an assessment of the possible risk factors for the physician and crew. Needless to say, if, under pressure, even a good commander like Escajeda could put me in harm's way by mistake and not think much of it, it appeared—and not for the first time—that in war we were all of little consequence.

And some were of even less consequence than others. I was one of four General Medical Officers (GMOs) in the hospital unit, and we had the least advanced training of all the physicians. In other words, I was particularly expendable. I knew that Escajeda had a difficult job, and that he had personally treated several doctors wounded on helicopter trips to dangerous places. One surgeon in particular had sustained a serious gunshot wound in the abdomen while coming off a helicopter at a remote hospital near the demilitarized zone (DMZ) between North and South Vietnam. I also knew that I was being sent closer to the fighting than I had ever been, and felt some pride that I was thought capable of replacing Waldron. Yet I had hoped—irrationally, I knew—that I could spend the rest of my tour at C Med, which was already closer to the shooting than I wanted to be.

At C Med we treated Marines being flown in by helicopter from combat, managing as well as we could in our old World War II tents, clustered around two operating rooms and an intensive care unit (ICU). These wounded Marines never stayed for long; we shipped them off to the hospital at Clark Air Base in the Philippines once they were stable enough to fly, and as our beds were being filled. In some cases, the distance to C Med was too far from combat, and Marines died on their way to us. So the "shock unit"—a new experiment—was an innovative concept in treating casualties. It was hoped that placing the unit nearer to the action in the Harvest Moon operation would lower the death rate. I understood the logic, and I understood it would likely result in more wounded doctors.

The ride to Harvest Moon would be my first real view of the inland countryside. I climbed into the helicopter, and was seated between the two open side-doors, each manned by a remarkably calm crewman in charge of a mounted 50-caliber machine gun. The engine roar and the blade beat were deafening. I grabbed the central stanchion so I wouldn't fall out when the ship banked. My bowel responded by cramping, and I became intensely aware of the possible unknowns of this flight into the battle zone.

The .45 revolver strapped on my hip gave me some comfort, but I hadn't previously thought through the idea of being in a situation where I actually would need to pull it out, point it, and fire at another human. As a doctor, and more particularly as a Quaker, shooting someone had been inconceivable in my life up to this point. Somehow I had let the incongruity of carrying a gun slip from the forefront of my mind with pitifully little soul-searching.

As we flew to the site I could see below us the thick canopy that covered the jungle floor. It was interrupted only by wide-open rice fields, some dotted with ten-foot circular structures that, from the air, looked like bomb craters. I later learned that they were Vietnamese family memorial markers.

Rain had been heavy in the monsoon months of October and November, leaving the fields filled with water. As we moved inland, I occasionally detected the thin line of a road emerging from the hillside growth. We were flying just hundreds of feet off the ground, barely above any potential ground fire. Thankfully, we were not in a military truck down on one of those roads, where Marines were blown up or ambushed daily. The enemy was down there—exactly where, we didn't know. They could be hidden in the jungle or dressed as civilians. My father, also a physician, had served in some of the worst fighting in Europe during World War II, and I knew that this was not his experience of war, in which the battle line had been distinct.

As we approached the Harvest Moon forward supply depot, where the medical tents were located, we dropped vertically, near two 105 howitzers that were firing with loud and rhythmic authority. Our destination was the center of a sandy, 200-acre clearing, most likely an ancient lakebed among the volcanic foothills. This is a sight that rarely occurs in mountainous central Vietnam. Canvas tarps covered piles of food and ammunition surrounding the triage area.

As I landed, I could see Waldron working on a Marine, putting final touches on a leg splint. I threw my bedroll into a nearby tent, and when I turned around, Waldron was already waving goodbye as he ran to the helicopter that would not wait.

So much for my briefing.

I didn't have time to worry what would happen next. No sooner had that helicopter taken off than another landed, delivering one severely wounded Marine on a stretcher and two others who could still walk. One of the GMOs and I teamed up to work on the stretcher case, a young man with a gaping chest wound. He was not speaking and his face had a gray pallor. He needed three things instantly: an intravenous (IV) insertion, a chest tube, and an endotracheal tube. Indeed, he had needed these things the second he had been hit, so now there was very little time to spare. A chest tube was inserted while I was working on an arm IV. Suddenly, the Marine stopped breathing. I managed to secure a femoral IV line, and by then my fellow GMO had inserted a tube in his airway. A corpsman started chest massage, which proved futile because the wounded man's vascular volume was so low.

The last possible option to save his life was to open his chest completely and temporarily clamp his aorta while replacing fluid loss. This maneuver would allow us to pump his heart manually. We knew that the procedure so rarely worked that it had been given up at C Med, except in cases of suspected cardiac injuries. Lacking an alternative, we tried nonetheless, but it was too late. His heart would not beat, and his pupils dilated in moments, indicating brain death. At C Med I had been working on Marines who had died, but there I had been a junior member of a large team. Here, I was the surgeon in charge. In painful silence, the other GMO and I avoided looking at each other.

Having one month's more experience than the others on the ground at Harvest Moon, I needed to be the one to keep a larger perspective than just the task in front of me. During a break in the proceedings at the end of that first day in the shock unit, after we had watched this patient being placed in a body bag, I took a moment to assess for myself the actual surroundings here, and the men with whom I had been working. We had one experienced corpsman who had been at B Med before Harvest Moon. He knew the routine and could think ahead, for instance, about chest tube placement equipment, the type of IV solution and the interior catheters that would be required. The rest of them had joined this team straight from the field, and had very different levels of skill from each other and, especially, from the one more seasoned corpsman from B Med. But they were learning fast.

It is a daunting responsibility to be presented with a young man who is so severely wounded that he is unconscious solely from blood loss, and just minutes from death. A single person alone cannot do all that is required, quickly enough. It takes a team of at least six people: doctors, corpsmen, and specially trained techs who all need to function together smoothly in order to be successful. Teamwork builds over time, with feedback and communication. Each case requires a designated leader who can assign tasks and be flexible enough to modify the plan as the situation changes. One indication that a team is working efficiently is if the team members can control their anxiety and speak normally. These were all things I had experienced back at C Med.

Our shock team at Harvest Moon was hastily thrown together, however, from two different hospitals, B Med and C

Med, with no prior experience working together. We worked under an open tent that held twenty stretchers. The wounded came to us in groups of two or three, often within thirty minutes of being wounded. The helicopter would wait for them while we started IVs, stabilized their breathing, and placed pressure dressings on bleeding wounds. They then would make the forty-minute trip either to C Med or to B Med, at Chui Lai, an hour south of Da Nang on the coast.

Time was always critical for the newly wounded. We three GMOs were now the ones to decide who might need a chest-tube insertion without taking the time for X-ray confirmation, and, if we missed the insertion of an arm IV, we had to decide whether or not to take precious time to do a surgical cut-down on an ankle vein (a surgical procedure taking ten minutes). Delay in proper care could lead to circulatory collapse or other fatal complications before the wounded Marine could reach the hospital.

We lacked sufficient supplies, personnel numbers, and more experienced doctors. All of us had been through medical school, internship, and had begun surgical training programs. But these were hardly résumés that would recommend us for a job this critical. We had become vastly more competent over the previous months at our respective units in Vietnam, but also wise enough to be frustrated by our shortcomings.

This group of corpsmen and the two doctors had been working now for twenty-four hours straight. In this quiet moment, I saw right away that these men were all badly fatigued, grubby, slumped over, and much in need of rest and sleep. Their clothing was bloody, and there was no way to change their clothing. They appeared almost beaten down, and I knew that they were badly shaken, as well, by the close gunfire that had broken out sporadically during the night, beyond the perimeter.

That Marine with the gaping chest wound was not the very first one that I had seen die. But when we lost him, I felt I had to say something to steady the others on our team, as well as myself. "He had a fatal injury. Let's not get down on ourselves. There are some things we could do differently." Despite everyone's fatigue, I knew I had their attention. These men were devoted to the task at hand, and were listening. "First of all, it was insane to open that chest forty minutes out from an OR. We are all in over our heads, and none of us has superior knowledge or skill, so let's just pull together as a team."

Within hours of losing that patient at Harvest Moon, we came under Viet Cong small-arms fire from the jungle several hundred yards away. I heard the distinct popping sound of the AK-47, which I had heard before, although never at such close range.

A corpsman yelled, "Hit the deck! Hit the deck! Put the stretchers on the ground!"

Each stretcher, of course, held a wounded patient. When I looked at the tree line, I could see the muzzle puffs. Everything happened too fast to be as frightening as it should have been. I joined the stretchers flat on the ground. I was so inexperienced that I had a sense of excitement mixed with fear, rather than fear alone. From my position in the sand, I watched with amazement as the Marines tasked with protecting us took up their rifles and hurried in zigzag patterns directly toward the hostile fire. This is standard operating procedure (SOP) for the Marines, who always take the offensive to avoid being pinned down. I was deeply impressed that these young men, without any hesitation, would put their lives at risk to protect us.

By sundown, I had seen enough to realize that our position was exposed and vulnerable. Surely we should have anticipated additional attacks. I remembered the flight in, when I had seen that our location was next to the ammunition resupply dump and helicopter refueling center for the entire Harvest Moon operation. This made us the perfect military target for the Viet Cong. The Marines, thinking the same, had focused two small tanks and three recoil-less rifles on the tree line around us. I remember thinking how strange it was that were it not for the constant combat, the area could have been labeled a scenic spot in the Pouch Ha Valley.

There were moments that day when I had a break from tending to the wounded. Thinking about my own safety and the potential need to be below ground in an attack, I started to dig a slit trench next to my bedroll. The two doctors from B Med brushed off my idea, especially when rain inundated our position and my trench collected six inches of water. But at 2200 hours that night, when the first Viet Cong mortar shells hit and we felt the ground shaking violently with each booming impact, they too scrambled into my water-filled trench. It felt to me that each one of us was trying to get lower than the other.

During the second day, we lost three more Marines, and during one four-hour period we ran out of the intravenous catheters, which we used for infusing large volumes of fluid. This was a procedure crucial for counteracting large losses of blood. Not knowing what else to do, I improvised (something I would get used to), grabbing some infusion tubing, cutting off the adapter end, and cutting down on the saphenous vein at the ankle, where the flexible tubing could then be threaded and secured with a ligature. It worked so well that we subsequently used the technique all year for big volume replacement needs. Supplies were uncertain. I was learning quickly that trial and error was often the only way.

When the Harvest Moon operation started, the war was nine months old. The fighting was heavier than had been anticipated in the hasty troop build-up that started in March 1965. (U.S. military numbers went from 27,000 to 184,000 in that year). In the early planning for the war, the Marine Corps had volunteered to man the I Corps (the northern tier of South Vietnam), where the largest concentration of enemy soldiers was located. In the rush of the buildup, though, neither the Marines nor the Navy, which was supplying medical personnel, had been fully prepared for what was needed. The equipment for the medical battalion of the 3rd Marine Division had been in mothballs for more than twenty years, literally since World War II, and the medical personnel generally did not have experience with, or full procedures in place for, the mass of casualties that was coming in.

For example, when I first arrived in Vietnam, I had never treated a gunshot wound. I had never seen what a young man looked like moments from death due to hemorrhage. Even the fully trained surgeons, who had been drafted just out of civilian surgical training, had never seen the severity of the wounds they now saw every day. So it was clear that all of us would have to learn on the fly. Even the experienced "regular Navy" surgeons in our unit had never worked in an actual war zone. In the overwhelming situations in which we found ourselves, it was absolutely necessary for all of us to find ways to stay calm and focus, so we could think clearly.

The three months of experience I'd had at C Med produced a veneer of confidence in me that was tested at Harvest Moon. Eventually, I came to realize that this experience would be critical to my maturation and evolution, as a person and as a surgeon. The efficacy of my own medical education was now coming to me in a great flood. In one twenty-four-hour stretch at Harvest Moon, our shock unit treated ninety wounded men.

At C Med, I had been good at handling the situation directly in front of me, but I had always been able also to turn to more experienced doctors for help or advice when I needed it. Now, at Harvest Moon, I had to assess the situation for myself and manage how best to use the talents we had. Which of these men were best at IVs, for instance? Who could do cutdowns or intubations better than others?

Also, until then, I had never sought out more responsibility than what others had handed me. After Harvest Moon, I began seeking out personal responsibility wherever I could find it. I had to. We all did. I understood then that we were working at the edge of dangerous uncertainty all the time, so danger and uncertainty were no longer allowable excuses for inaction on my part.

After four days and nights at Harvest Moon, the fighting slowed enough that it was deemed time for us to be shipped back to C Med. I joined a number of Marines in a twenty-truck caravan. Our three-doctor, eight-corpsman unit had treated 150 wounded Marines. We had been shelled twice and survived two perimeter attacks just yards from our working station. The idea of returning to C Med filled me with relief, and I then realized how much I had been suffering from an acid stomach throughout that four-day period.

As soon as we boarded the trucks, I relaxed and started to nod off with exhaustion. But, relieved as I was to leave the battle behind, I soon remembered that we were now on the road, and in Vietnam the road was not a safe place to be, especially when we were in a long, slow-moving convoy. I felt exposed to danger sitting in a truck that, if attacked, would be unable to escape forward or backward from the caravan. In Vietnam, I learned that just when you thought you were safe, you realized you weren't.

In those four days of Harvest Moon, we lost a number of Marines. But we had succeeded in saving those who had had a reasonable chance to be saved. I had learned how to work with precision to stop bleeding, to keep life from draining from a young body.

Bent over a chest or a leg wound, I had been able to block out my fear of where I was. Now, here on the open road, wedged into the truck's cab and in a rural setting probably dominated by Viet Cong, I was tense, on guard, and clearly couldn't rely on my professional ability to moderate my own fear.

I continued to wear the .45 revolver, although it was now clear to me it was just for show. I didn't know how to use it competently, and was still ambivalent about even having it. In fact, I probably would be safer with my hands up, surrendering, than pulling a gun. While I braced myself every time the trucks slowed, the Marines in the truck ahead of me, realizing they were much safer than they had been in weeks, laughed and called out to each other. They were headed away from tense combat toward base camp, and for them the trucks offered relative safety, the promise of a short rest, and maybe a shower at the other end.

I briefly envied them their sense of safety, until I remembered the price they had paid, or would pay, for it. In the next days or weeks—or maybe even in the next few minutes—I might have my hands deep inside one of their chests, trying to staunch the bleeding or closing off a stump above his knee. I didn't know how any of us would return to normal after this. I wasn't ready to admit it to myself yet, but the life we had thought of as normal—in my case, growing up in Iowa in the 1950s—had been left behind and could not be returned to.

At one point on the ride home, we pulled to a stop. The convoy was stretched out single-file in a village, surrounded by hundreds of Vietnamese. Many of the men carried automatic weapons over their shoulders. Some of them looked like the South Vietnamese soldiers of the ARVN, but I couldn't be sure, and I knew that, in any case, the ARVN was heavily infiltrated with Viet Cong. Alarmed, I thought, *Is this a planned ambush or is there a cow or something else up the road?* I knew we couldn't even be halfway to Da Nang; there was no good reason to stop here.

The Marines in the truck ahead of me jumped out of their vehicle, and I crouched down, thinking that they had discovered, with their feral instincts for danger, an imminent attack. Their weapons were slung, however, and they were smiling and shoving at each other. They encircled a scraggly pine tree on the side of the road, and one of the Marines took out his trenching tool and hacked away at the trunk until the tree toppled over. They cheered. Two of the Marines lifted the tree over their heads, and they carted it back to the truck. The villagers looked on in silence, not understanding what was happening.

"Our Christmas tree!" someone in the truck yelled. I had forgotten. It was December 20th, and at that moment Christmas could not have been further from my thoughts. Most of these Marines were just out of high school. Wiry and tanned, they seemed as fragile as schoolboys, yet I knew that they were more courageous than I would ever be. I had seen the results of the wounds that many of them would most probably sustain, and I hoped I was as good a doctor as they deserved.

Some time after Harvest Moon, the leadership at C Med and the Naval hospital in Da Nang evaluated the efficiency of the shock unit experiment. They invited Professor Ben Eisman, who was then Chairman of Surgery at the University of Kentucky, to Da Nang. He was a Korean War veteran and a captain in the Navy Reserve.

Dr. Eisman and the C Med leadership understood as well as anyone that the saving of the greatest number of wounded soldiers is the very heart of the moral dilemma for any medical team in war. They ultimately decided that the benefits of the shock unit were outweighed by the costs of slowing the transit of other casualties to the surgical hospital.

The shock unit model was therefore abandoned.

CHAPTER II

Indianola, Iowa

Farmers can smell the rain before it falls. The sky over my home in Indianola, Iowa in May of 1945 might well have been full with the fast-moving thunderheads that can coalesce at any moment into a dark approaching storm. The war in Europe would soon end. Ho Chi Minh, long the organizer of a Vietnam that he hoped would be free of outside control, was fighting against the Japanese occupation, with his band of loyalists and—ironically—with U.S. help.

During World War II, my father had been away for three years, in both the Pacific and European theaters. On one particular day when I was six, I was riding my tricycle up the sidewalk on North C Street, where we lived. I had been told not to cross any of the roads that surrounded our street, but I encountered a gathering of somber adults across the dirt road near the spruce tree that we called "the Christmas tree." While people have always been neighborly in small-town Iowa, they were especially so during the war. With gas rationing, adults walked more and visited each other, and looked after families whose men had gone to war. I sensed that there was something unusual, though, in this particular gathering, and I crossed the road.

The most fascinating man in the group had a giant purple, velvety protrusion on his face. I knew him, and he had seen my interest in his birthmark, even once letting me feel its warmth.

But not on this day. He turned to me and said, "Young man, President Roosevelt has died, and you must go tell your mother." Since I had been told that, with my father's absence, I was the man of the house, I felt important taking the message home. I usually stopped in the overgrown vacant lot between our house and the dirt road, in a little grove of plum trees that offered a secure hideout. But not today. I hurried home and found my mother in the kitchen, weeping. She had already heard the news.

Many years later, I read in David McCullough's book *Truman* that (as had been stated in private Allied messages), President Franklin Delano Roosevelt had strongly opposed the insertion of colonial power in the world, and therefore was not in favor of the reinsertion of French power in Indochina after the end of World War II. Colonial rule did not fit American values at the time. In addition the president was still disgruntled with the French Vichy army's resisting the Allied landing in North Africa in 1942.

Roosevelt's relationship with Vice President Harry Truman was such that he had not shared many of his ideas with Truman in the brief eighty-two days of Truman's vice-presidency. After the end of the war, Truman bowed to the threat of Communism, and allowed the reoccupation of Indochina by the French, which set up the events leading to the French-Indochina War that ultimately precipitated U.S. involvement in Vietnam.

In the 1940s and 50s, Indianola was a typical small county seat in Iowa, an uneventful township of about five thousand people. The courthouse stood in the center of the business district square. There were a few grocery stores, banks, jewelry stores, and pool halls that sold beer. In those days, respectable people didn't enter the pool halls—at least not through the front doors. Elm trees dominated the courthouse lawn and lined all the streets. The only stop light was at the intersection of the two highways that ran through the town.

My father was one of three doctors caring for the people of the town and the surrounding county. He had grown up on his parents' hundred-acre farm a half mile from Indianola, where my grandmother still lived. During World War II, my sister and I lived with her for a summer. My grandmother, preferring a simple life, still drove to town in a horse and buggy, to trade cream and eggs for staples and cash. My father was on the school board, and my mother was an active civic leader. Everyone in town knew our family, my two sisters, and our dog Buster, who visited us often at recess time on the schoolyard.

Each side of C Street, where we lived, was lined with giant elm trees, the branches of which arched across the pavement to meet their neighbor branches from the other side, thus forming a tunnel of shade. My grandmother always commented on the abundance of trees because, when she had been a five-year-old living southeast of Indianola, the prairie around her home had been treeless. The crossroad to the north of our house was simple dirt, and just two blocks to the west was the beginning of farmland. An occasional goat or horse would get loose and wander down C Street, giving my sisters and me reason to go out and watch. The way to school led two blocks south, through the park and across the Simpson College campus.

On her first day of kindergarten, my older sister insisted on my walking with her, to help protect her from any unleashed neighborhood dogs. We would walk together as far as the park, establishing the standard for walking to school that lasted for me, both my sisters, and friends through high school, no matter the weather.

The town was "protected" by two untrained police officers. Most homes and all bikes remained unlocked.

The year I was five, on one of our frequent walks with Mom to the park, my sisters (at the time aged four and six) and I saw a dead squirrel in the middle of the street. I was immensely curious, since I had never touched a squirrel before, or even seen a dead creature of any kind. I now think that my mother showed considerable thoughtfulness by allowing me to pick up the squirrel and to see how stiff and lifeless it was. I was not to poke it. We brought it home and buried it with a ceremony. In this one teaching moment, my sisters and I learned the risk of fast moving cars, the great divide between life and death, and a proper respect for all creatures, even in death.

I might have forgotten about the squirrel if not for a second event five years later, when I was ten. I had come home from school for lunch. Rarely did Dad get home to join us, but this autumn day was a fortunate exception. His blue 1947 Ford sedan was in the driveway in front of the house. Halfway through the meal, our neighbor Mrs. Shipper came to the screen door calling, "Doctor! Doctor!" She lived only two houses away, and was a very shy woman. She had never been to our door before. But just from her demeanor, I knew that something was wrong even before she announced that Bucky Small had been hit by a car. Dad asked me to bring his medical bag from the car, and he ran with Mrs. Shipper to the scene a block away. I snatched up the bag and ran behind them.

When I got there, Mrs. Small, who was a single mother, and seemed much older than my own mother, was on her porch, rocking her limp six-year-old boy and wailing, "Bucky, oh my Bucky." Dad could see that the boy was breathing, and placed him flat on the ground, noting that all four of his extremities were flaccid and that he was not responding to verbal or physical stimuli. Next, I watched as he looked at Bucky's eyes, listened to his heart and lungs, noted the boy's severe head hematoma (that to me as a ten year-old looked like a large goose egg), and looked for extremity fractures.

"Mrs. Shipper, call an ambulance. He needs to be in a Des Moines hospital at once. And Mrs. Small, as you can see, your boy is alive, but gravely ill with a head injury." I witnessed my generally reserved Dad step up that day in Bucky's front yard, as he directed and calmed neighbors and friends who wanted to help. He spoke quietly, preparing several of the neighbors for how serious Bucky's injury was. Dad asked for a volunteer to take Mrs. Small to the hospital. Someone immediately stepped forward and did as he asked.

Looking back years later, I realized that Dad's experience as a physician had told him that the case was more than likely hopeless, once he had noted Bucky's fixed and dilated pupils as well as the coma that had resulted from the accident. But in that moment, Dad betrayed none of what he knew. In a calm voice, he explained to Mrs. Small where the Methodist Hospital emergency room was, and that he needed to get on the phone to arrange for a neurosurgeon to meet him there.

Bucky died on the way to the hospital. It would be twenty-five years before ambulances in the U.S. were regularly outfitted with trained medical personnel and equipment for emergency situations. And it was almost twenty years later that I myself was in that same role, dealing with a fatal injury on the battlefield.

After Bucky Small's death was announced, neighbors divided up the preparing of meals and other ways to support the inconsolable mother. Like most people unaccustomed to tragic death, I stayed away from her door when I was out selling fundraising tickets. Indeed, I did not see Mrs. Small outside her house again for years. The tragedy seemed to have put up an unnecessary and hurtful wall between her and the rest of the town. It took many years before I learned myself what to say or do when I was in the presence of someone suffering such a loss.

After my father had returned from the war, he had often taken me with him on house calls. We never went up to the front door of the house. Rather we were always welcomed through the kitchen door, a privilege to us since this was where family and close friends would enter. In that era, before pagers, answering machines and, of course, cell phones, hardly a meal would pass in our house without a phone call from a patient. If Dad's car were in the driveway, it meant that he was home, and people came right up to the door when they needed to speak to him.

One evening, a farmer came to the house with his young son, who had suffered a fracture-dislocation of his elbow. Dad told the father to hold his son's chest and arm as he manually reduced the misalignment and placed a splint on it. Everyone had forgotten that my collie Buster was watching. When the boy let out a yell, Buster lunged at the boy's father and bit him on the arm. Dad treated the dog bite as well, giving the farmer instructions on wound care as well as a tetanus booster shot. I remember Dad saying as they were leaving, "Keep that arm elevated and come to the office in the morning for an X-ray." He gave a quick look of disapproval at Buster. "And there will be no charge for caring for either patient."

Buster was never again invited to be a member of the consultation team. The next day, the farmer announced that a quarter of beef would be delivered to our food locker, adding "That's quite a dog you have there."

My parents were not just the guardians of my childhood; they were trusted and respected mentors to me, with whom I could discuss values, decisions and a philosophy of life. Both had been raised in Quaker homes, had gone to Quaker colleges and lived with the tenet that there was "that of God" in every person. Since it's founding in 1650, The Religious Society of Friends, (whose members are informally known as Quakers) have been deeply interested in social justice, and opposed to war.

As a family, we ate together every day and had a silent grace before each meal. There was as well a family discussion every

Thursday evening, which made us aware of what it meant to be Quaker. The Quakerism that I was taught in our home, in a small town without an organized silent meeting, was centered on the theme of living a life of service. My father's role as a small-town doctor was emblematic of that idea. As well, before marrying my father, my mother, as a trained dietician, had led an American Friends Service Committee team in the clothing and feeding of starving children, in Kentucky and West Virginia coal mine camps, during the early years of The Depression.

We were taught a broad and respectful understanding of many of the great religions and cultures of the world. As well, we learned of specific local involvements that supported these teachings: for example, that George Washington Carver, an African American who had made major contributions to scientific agriculture, had attended our local Simpson College. Simpson is an institution founded by the United Methodist Church, and was in this case supported by the local Quakers for its inclusion of African American students like Carver. Dad and his siblings knew which Indianola Quaker farms had served on the Underground Railroad in the Civil War.

In 1946, a Jewish couple, the Risemans, refugees from the war, moved into a small upstairs apartment across the street from our house. My parents had lived in such a modest place when Dad had first started his practice. Mrs. Riseman was a talented musician, and Mom used her own considerable clout in town to get our new neighbor started in the teaching of private and group music lessons. My mother not only gave friendship to these new—and war traumatized—people; she also helped them find temporary livelihoods. Mrs. Riseman was finally able to establish her profession as a music teacher. I never heard a mention of anti-Semitism in our town. On the contrary, the Risemans' Jewish heritage made them special in our eyes.

The Quakers place much importance on the notions of generosity and forgiveness. In 1946, Germany was badly destroyed, as Dad had seen firsthand during the last days of the war, when his hospital unit had crossed Germany into Austria. Through the American Friends Service Committee, our family adopted families in Munich and Cologne—the Wimbergers and the Zylkas—and we sent them monthly care packages of clothing, and scarcities such as coffee and chocolate. The relationships continued after their acute need had passed, and culminated in our family visiting them in their homes in Germany in 1956. They also visited us in Iowa several years later.

On summer days, between baseball games and jobs baling hay at nearby farms, mowing yards, or sacking groceries, my friends and I often took the school bus five miles to Lake Ahquabi to swim. Because I went on house calls with my father, my friends called me "Doc." I was a good student. I respected my parents and my elders, and I trusted the world that I had come to know. As a young student, my path forward in life became clear to me: I would go to a Quaker college and, after four years, attend medical school and become a doctor.

Earlham College in Richmond, Indiana greatly broadened my knowledge. True to its Quaker affiliation, its curriculum focused on personal growth, rigorous intellectual honesty and service to others. The faculty was accessible to all of us, and the teachers made wonderful role models. It was common to have lunch with our math professor, Clifford Crump, and to hear the thoughts and concerns of other faculty in our Quaker meetings. Mindful of my medical future, I worked part-time nights and weekends as a lab tech at Reid Hospital in Richmond, Indiana.

On one of my visits home, Dad put me to work during an emergency night call. The patient was a small-time farmer who was making a very simple living, having spent his productive years as a foreign missionary. He lived alone, and called Dad one night after midnight. He felt the need to apologize. He had tried to wait until morning, but the abdominal pain and vomiting he had endured had become more than he could stand. This kind of waiting to the last moment was typical of Dad's small-town clientele, many of whom were farmers. They explained that they understood that my father worked long hours, and that they wished to protect him. From what this particular farmer said over the phone, Dad assumed that he would find a condition requiring surgery.

We picked up Dad's microscope from his office, and then drove the five miles to the farmer's house, largely on dirt roads. There was probably no one in the county who knew these roads better than Dad. We let ourselves in to the farmhouse's back door, and found our patient in bed, weak with shallow, jagged breathing. The sweat of sepsis beaded on his forehead. His skin bore the unhealthy tint of jaundice, and he had a tender, rigid belly. With my father's instructions, I was able to do the lab work on the kitchen table, and told Dad that our patient had a high white blood cell count and that he tested positive for bile in his urine. In the hospital two hours later, Dad helped the surgeon, Tom Throckmorton, remove a leaking gangrenous gall bladder.

I scrubbed as an observer.

Near the end of the case, Dad said to the surgeon, "Tom, this man has meager savings and might lose his little farm if there is a big bill. He's lived a generous life, so I won't charge him myself." It seems to me now that this was a time, at least in Indianola, when people knew and cared for each other. My father knew the life circumstances of most of the families whose farms we passed, and therefore, he knew who needed a break in the usual fee.

In those days everyone we knew in Iowa was against the idea of "socialized medicine," and "socialism" in general, yet that generation of family doctors did not question which patients could pay before helping them. The custom for physicians was to bill on a sliding scale based on the patient's wealth. My father, and the other doctors we knew, helped everyone who needed care.

CHAPTER III

Medical School, September 1959

I was in a rush to become a doctor, and after three years at Earlham, I applied for early admission to Stanford University Medical School in Palo Alto, California. Stanford had a certain draw in our family because my cousin Oliver Thomas had gone to medical school there, and my uncle Elton Trueblood had been Chaplain and Professor of Philosophy at the university. I was accepted, and left Indianola with warnings from my eighty-five-year-old grandmother of the dangers of city life. I was not to date a Catholic, my grandmother said, or to stand on automobile running boards. She was not aware that in 1959, cars no longer had running boards. She insisted on sewing $20.00 into my clothing, in case I was robbed on the train or in San Francisco.

Managing alone on the farm for years, Grandma was so fearless in many ways that, for example, she still climbed up and fixed the windmill if it were broken, by herself. But the unknown and imagined dangers of the west coast alarmed her. I rode the train from Des Moines, 2,000 miles to the Palo Alto station, got off the train and walked down the palm-lined road to the center of the Stanford campus, carrying my large suitcase and my microscope.

In 1959, Stanford's medical school (which had for years been primarily in San Francisco) had just moved to new buildings on the Stanford campus, with a greatly expanded basic science faculty. One of the most prominent professors was Dr. Arthur Kornberg, who had just won the Nobel Prize for his work with DNA synthesis, and who had brought his department to Stanford from Washington University in St. Louis. The biochemistry lectures were so good and so revelatory of new developments in the field that that they were attended by the larger faculty as well. The department members were all leaders in molecular biology, and two more department members were later recognized as Nobel Laureates. Stanford was not the only center for such DNA research, of course, but the magic of DNA's synthesis and replication transformed the entire field of medicine.

I was hired the summer after my freshman year to work in the biochemistry lab under the direction of Dr. David Hoagness. There, I was buried in a world of test tubes, incubators, and centrifuges, with the assignment of growing a large batch of viruses, the genes of which could be transmitted from one bacteria to another. But while the research work was fascinating and the department conferences intellectually stimulating, I missed working with people.

I had signed an early admission agreement with Stanford that stipulated that I finish my undergraduate degree in the first three years, in addition to taking the scheduled classes in biochemistry, anatomy, physiology, pharmacology, and histology, as well as physical diagnosis. The load was all-consuming, and basically eliminated time for anything else. Indeed, I missed the television coverage of the Cuban missile crisis until its very last moments, as well as, more generally, the music, television shows, and other news reports of the time.

In my third year of medical school, we started clinical rotations. Dr. Jake Hanbury was Chief of Neurosurgery at Stanford, and his was the first clinical service in which I took part. We were a team of four students, all of us novices to actual patient care. Hanbury had a short leg, and wore a shoe with

24

a six-inch heel. The right side of his face was paralyzed, and often a pipe hung from his droopy mouth.

His intensely somber personality mirrored the great professional burden he was carrying. My memory of his patient load was that most of them either had incurable cancer or were children born with enormous heads, the result of neglected hydrocephalus. All they could be offered from medicine at that time was a shunt to arrest the growing head. It was too late to preserve normal brain function. On the second day of rounds, Dr. Hanbury took us to a scheduled meeting with the mother of one of the children with hydrocephalus, and bluntly spelled out to her how her child was doomed to an institutionalized life with a feeding tube. Indeed, we were as shaken as was the mother.

After the conference, Hanbury kept us in the room, surveyed our stricken demeanor, and said, "Look, I did not ask you to do this work; if you can't handle the hard parts, you'd best quit now." We did not see ourselves as quitters. But from that moment we were greatly sobered by the limitations of our chosen field.

This was not my first encounter with a suffering patient or with the difficult aspects of a physician's job. I had seen my father deliver bad news and confront hopeless cases, but Dr. Hanbury's advice seemed to suggest that our chosen profession would require us to become calloused. I therefore walked away from the woman and her child with a heavy heart. I had wanted to go into medicine so that I could support and help people. Perhaps Dr. Hanbury had still had compassion for patients and families during his own training decades earlier, but it seemed to me that, if so, he had emptied the well, and I tried to attribute this to a specialty that, at the time, offered few happy outcomes.

One of my senior residents offered some great advice that day: "You can learn how to be a physician just as fast by watching situations handled poorly, as when it is done perfectly."

I called my Dad in Iowa that night and asked him how he gave bad news to families. "First, I would ask her to have her family or friends come in, for an in-depth discussion in which there would be a lot to remember. I would then sit down with all of them and warn them that this would be a difficult conversation. Then I would encourage the mother that her baby needs her, that she has an important job to do, and that she will have to discover how to do it in her own way." This is advice that, depending on the particular circumstances, I've followed ever since.

While at Stanford, I held a part-time job as lab assistant for Dr. Harry Oberhelman, who ran the physiology lab. He was using dogs as experimental animals to define the relative role of hormones and the nervous system in digestion. Soon I was doing technical surgery on these animals under the direction of Bob Mason, Dr. Oberhelman's resident. My main job was to check on, feed, and test the dogs. But one weekend I found a very sick animal. He was vomiting and had a rigid abdomen. Mason was not available. I had learned enough to take the animal to the laboratory, anesthetize it, and open the abdomen. I thought I would find a bowel obstruction. Instead, I found that the animal had been nervously eating his own shed hair, which had formed a tight solid ball (hair bezoar) that obstructed the outlet of his stomach. It was a simple matter to open the stomach, remove the bezoar and repair the opening, and I was gratified to be able to relieve the suffering of another living creature so directly and immediately. I felt encouraged to have been of service, yet it probably reenforced the false sense young surgeons have that they will always be able to save the patient.

During the summer break that year, on the long drive back to Iowa, I stopped at the ranch of Dan and Elizabeth Jensen in Wyoming, a 10,000-acre spread near Chugwater, where I had worked for three months before starting medical school. Elizabeth was a Quaker woman whom Dad had known in Philadelphia while in medical school. My mother knew her also, through her American Friends Service Committee connections. The Jensens had become good friends of mine, too, from that past summer.

Soon after I arrived, John, the hired man, found a cow with a prolapsed uterus. Her calf was not being nursed because she was so sick. Dan and John thought that, since I was now in medical school and had operated on dogs, I could do anything a veterinarian could do. They reminded me how, three summers before, I had treated a Hereford bull with pinkeye. (To treat the bull, I had gone daily into the corral alone with the animal, looped a rope over his horns and pulled them tight to a post where he could not move his head, then forced open each eye to apply antibiotic cream.)

It is true that young surgeons are often more bold than they have reason to be, and on that day I did fit that label. I was thinking that I might as well try to do something for the cow with the prolapsed uterus. I liked the adventure, and I knew we could call a vet as a backup. We ran her into a chute, gave her a close approximation of an epidural anesthesia and cleaned most of the maggots off the shaggy, swollen uterus, leaving behind a few maggots to clean up any dead tissue. I then returned the uterus to her abdomen and, with a big needle and shoelace-size suture, secured it. With daily penicillin shots and some good luck, she resumed nursing.

These surgeries were minor in importance by comparison to the experiences I would have later in Da Nang. But I know now that they instilled confidence in me, so that even these proved key to my experiences there, when I found myself in situations that were over my head and in which I had to innovate.

Each Christmas break during medical school, I worked with Dad in his office and on house calls. I remember one call, when the day-night/freeze-thaw cycle had left a slippery glaze on the roadbed. Driving on it was like driving on six inches of jelly atop the frozen ground. The last half-mile required driving fast enough to make forward progress, but not so rapidly that we would slip into a ditch.

The patient we had come to see was a thirty-five-year-old woman whose thyroid cancer had metastasized into her brain, causing a paralysis of her left side. My father was talking with her husband, listening to the husband's report of a recent trip they had made to the University Hospital in Iowa City. I was waiting in the next room with our patient, and she asked me, "Am I going to die?" Then, after a silence, "What's going to happen to me?" At her husband's request, the doctors and nurses at University Hospital had not been free to discuss this with her.

The skill of handling such questions comes with experience and the ability to anticipate the patient's willingness to hear the simple truth. Talking to a terminal patient is different than telling someone sad news about a loved one. One form of this encounter is to give a little of the answer and see whether more information is truly wanted. I knew, in the case of this conversation, that I was in way over my head, yet I felt her listening intensely for my answer. I could see her newly weak arm as she nervously picked up one hand with the other and dropped it like a dead weight into her lap. Her loving and protective husband was leaving her out of the most vital information of her life, and she was clearly frustrated. Recalling my experience of Dr. Hanbury's methods, I knew enough not to be blunt, and I had listened to my father's advice on how to handle these conversations, but I'd never put it into practice before. I started slowly: "When a tumor spreads from the neck to the brain, it is usually very serious."

Her husband overheard us, and became immediately furious. Rage, frustration, and confusion burned in equal proportions in his eyes, and I thought how much easier and smarter it would have been to simply plead ignorance, and to wait for my father to return from the next room. My father now had to negotiate with an overwhelmed husband and his wife, each desperate for hope and truth. I knew, even before I saw the expression on my father's face, that I had created more trouble than I knew how to fix. He straightened his back and told the couple that the situation was not hopeless because the university wanted to try an experimental use of radioactive iodine.

As we drove home, my father said nothing about my mistake. But I already knew I would be more careful in the future. I hoped that he would offer me some wisdom, and I wondered if I had misapplied his prior advice, but we continued in silence, as was often the case with my father. I was left to contemplate the example of his actions without fully understanding what had led to them. In this particular case, he hadn't told the patient a lie; there was still hope. Surely, though, there wasn't much hope, and I wondered whether Dad's words were more for the husband than for his wife. I would have to negotiate these conversations on my own in the coming years, and there was often no clear path.

When I returned to Stanford that summer, one of my rotations was on the cardiac surgical service headed by Dr. Norman Shumway. For the previous two years, my part time job in Dr. Oberhelman's lab had been just a few doors from Dr. Shumway's heart lab. In that close-knit group, I had a chance to learn from the soon-to-be famous innovator of heart transplantation.

He would occasionally drop in to the lab where I was working, and subject me to specific questions. "What is the tidal volume setting on your anesthesia machine? What would happen to the animal's heart if you doubled the respiration rate and cut the volume in half?" He was challenging me to think about basic physiology.

Shumway also loved to laugh, play jokes, and tell off-color

stories. He called me "Ward-o," as Commander Escajeda later would, and joked about my long distance running. "You know, don't you, that on the back of every heart is a stenciled number—the number of beats for the lifetime of that heart. Don't you think by exercising that you are using up beats and shortening your life?" And then off he would go, leaving me without a good response.

Shumway had a serious side, though, and his surgical results were superior. One of the cases to which I was assigned as a student was that of a teenage boy with a congenital hole between two chambers of his heart. The aim of the procedure was to open the beating heart and repair the hole with a patch. It was my job to sew up the skin. I was close to finishing the procedure when the scrub nurse discovered a nut was missing from the sternal spreader that was used to keep the split breastbone apart during the open-heart section. We took an X-ray, and found that the nut was lying behind the heart. Shumway had left the OR for the day, but was called back. He asked his chief resident what he would do. The resident said we would have to reopen the sternum and remove the nut.

Shumway then asked the ethical question, "Do we notify the family?" He then answered his own question. "Yes. Give me the film, and I will show them the picture while you remove the nut."

Until my last year at Stanford, I assumed I would go into general surgery because it fit the surgical skills I had learned in Oberhelman's lab. I loved the "hands-on" action. I also loved working on the whole body as my field. However, in late 1963 I took an elective clerkship with Dr. Henry Kaplan, chief of Radiation Therapy. At the time he was the most renowned clinician at Stanford. Dr. Kaplan was a big man, and his focus on his work, the breadth of his knowledge and his intense eyes made him seem an even larger personality. He was instrumental in the development of the field of modern radiation therapy and in demonstrating the long-term survival of previously fatal cancers, like Hodgkin's disease. I wanted to involve myself in the exciting developments in this new field. When Kaplan said, "Ward, I want you on my team," I could not say no, and I soon committed to residency training with him.

One of Kaplan's great skills was to include the medical students, even the lowest in seniority, in clinical conferences. These teaching sessions were held impromptu after the team of senior residents in oncology and radiation therapy had presented a new patient to him. Kaplan had the knack of engaging students in the discussion of issues dealing with this particular illness in ways that did not place them in any sort of uncomfortable moment of embarrassment. He might ask, "How would you design a study to confirm your hypothesis that the disease is caused by a virus?" In answering that question the student could feel some sense of competence without having to know all the specific details. Yet Kaplan was not easy on a senior resident who might not have noted an enlarged lymph node, or had missed asking about any prior history of infectious mononucleosis. He was, without a doubt, one of the national leaders in applying real scientific principles to the treatment of a specific disease, in this case Hodgkin's disease, which he felt should be universally curable.

Kaplan also showed that there was a caring side to his driven personality. My third-year roommate, Steve Youman, was ill with T-cell lymphoma of the chest cavity. Kaplan brought Steve into his own home and oversaw his treatment throughout his long illness. During the last year of his life, Steve demonstrated a passion verging on desperation to finish his goal of becoming a doctor. He would work to exhaustion and then end up in bed for a week, only to repeat that sequence. Steve did not live to see his goal, but he inspired the rest of us never to take our good fortune—our health—lightly.

At that time I became subject to the military draft, and I

requested a deferment, so that I could finish my three-year residency training at Stanford in radiation therapy. The deferment allowed both the young doctors and the administrators of the various training programs the assurance that the doctors could finish specialty training before they served in the military.

Although one might be accepted for residency in radiation therapy, a preliminary year in a general medical internship was required to become a practicing physician. I was fortunate to meet the requirements of the Hospital of the University of Pennsylvania (HUP), a highly regarded institution. I had spent part of the previous year working as a senior medical student at Bellevue in New York City, and wanted more of the east coast medical experience.

My internship at HUP was split: half on medicine services, half on surgical services. I thought the blend of medicine and surgical training would be a good basis for either a career in radiation oncology or surgery. The more time I spent in surgery, the more I knew that I liked the challenge of both day and night care of the sickest patients, the ones so often seen in general surgery, patients who could be saved only by timely surgery. Radiation therapy rarely had the same direct and immediate feedback that surgery provided.

Early in my year at HUP, Dr. William Fitz was the attending surgeon on the resident-run service for indigent patients, where I was an intern. One day on rounds, we encountered a young patient who had right lower-quadrant pain, abdominal muscle guarding, and an elevated white-cell count, all signs and symptoms of appendicitis. Before the attending physician arrived, we placed this young man on the schedule for urgent surgery that day. Fitz seized the teaching moment, pulled up a chair and sat at the bedside, looked at the patient's abdomen, and proceeded to get his own history from the patient. The attending surgeon of the previous week had simply rubber stamped our decisions. Fitz, however, became actively involved, and extracted a fine point from the patient's history: the patient could tell the exact moment the pain started, whereas appendicitis usually starts slowly. This revelation was much more consistent with a diagnosis of a perforated stomach ulcer. After very carefully running his fingers over the belly and percussing the abdomen, he pointed out what we had missed. "This man has a perforated stomach ulcer, which has leaked down the right peritoneal gutter, and a film will show free air in the abdominal cavity."

We obtained the film, and Fitz was proven right. While the patient had described tenderness in the right lower quadrant, which had led to our diagnosis of acute appendicitis, we had not attended to the lack of motion and the guarding of the entire abdomen, which signified diffuse abdominal infection, more consistent with a perforation.

In Fitz, we had watched a master clinician. If we had proceeded with our planned appendectomy, we would have missed the perforated duodenal ulcer and, so, could have put the patient's life at risk. By sitting down and getting the precise medical story, and using his skill at physical examination, Fitz had given us a great lesson. That scene was almost magical to me. This was why I had gone to medical school: to possess the wisdom and skill to save someone's life.

Surgery, with its combination of diagnosis, intervention, and healing, was now my dream job, and it has remained so all my professional life. I learned early on that surgeons, like everyone, could be imperfect, contradictory, and complex. Fitz himself was physically rotund. He smoked and was short of breath on stairs. He sweat enough in the OR that a nurse was assigned to stand behind him holding a cold damp towel, to keep his forehead sweat from dripping into the open incision. But he was one of my best teachers.

I was encouraged and given responsibility by the HUP surgery staff, including the chief of surgery, Dr. Jonathan Rhoads.

Rhoads had authored a textbook of surgery, and was a kind and thoughtful mentor for me. That year, he conceived of the idea that patients with injured or diseased intestines might heal faster if relieved of eating for several months. The question he posed was, "Could patients be fed adequate nourishment intravenously during the gut's rest period?" Two of my co-residents, Doug Wilmore and Stan Dudrick, took this project to the laboratory and, by working with experimental animals, proved that indeed they could be adequately fed in such a way. (This discovery was a major advancement in medicine, and, years later, after my time in Vietnam, I would become involved in the early clinical trials that established the feasibility and safety of this new type of feeding, which allowed for faster, safer, and more efficient recovery. I was exhilarated to be part of such a novel change in medicine.)

Rhoades offered me a surgical residency on March 1, 1965, which would include two years at HUP and a final two years at Philadelphia General Hospital. I accepted, and notified Dr. Kaplan at Stanford of my change in plans. He expressed his disappointment, but he was supportive.

My decision came six months after the Gulf of Tonkin resolution of August 1964, and before President Lyndon Johnson ordered the first Marine landing near Da Nang in Vietnam.

In changing my specialty, I lost my draft deferment, which had been contingent on finishing radiation therapy at Stanford, just when the country was about to go to war. For the first time in years, the Navy decided to draft two hundred doctors. Before Vietnam, doctors were rarely drafted. Dr. Rhoades believed that I would be more valuable to the Navy as a fully trained surgeon, and wrote letters on my behalf. However, the Navy wanted me right away and, although a Quaker, I was off to war.

While I had been an undergraduate at Earlham College, there had been three men on campus who had gone to jail for not registering for the draft because of their deep conviction, based in the teachings of the Quaker faith, that war is wrong. I had not personally known people before who acted out their belief with such conviction. None of these men had made an issue or speeches about what they had done, but we all knew they had made a mature and thoughtful decision based on principles requiring decisive action.

Quakers have a long history of being conscientious objectors. In the Civil War and World Wars I and II, many would perform alternative service as ambulance drivers.

At first, I thought it was unfair to be the only one from my high school class, all of us now twenty-seven years old, who remained eligible for the draft simply because I had chosen medicine as a field of study and a profession. But I quickly changed my attitude.

I admired my Dad and his service in the Army. As he had explained to me, during World War II, draft boards required each rural county in Iowa to provide two doctors to the war effort. Dad was by far the youngest physician practicing in Warren County, and he felt obliged to step forward. He was thirty-six. He reasoned that if he claimed conscientious objector status, it would then force a fifty-year-old physician colleague to serve in his place. Also, given that the role of the physician would be free of combat action, my father felt comfortable becoming a battlefield doctor.

I felt the same. Also, all my mentors said that war-zone surgery would be more valuable than many years of civilian hospital training. Few of them had actually ever been to a war zone, but that didn't concern me at the time. Knowing that I would be advancing my surgery skills was motivation enough, and that added to the drive that pushes many young people: the desire to prove that I could do what I thought of as "the hard stuff" in life.

CHAPTER IV

Draft Notice—Camp Pendleton, July-August 1965

I was newly in love.

Nancy was a nurse at HUP, when I was an intern and surgical resident. We had met in September 1964 on a blind date. She had worked at Massachusetts General Hospital in Boston, after graduating from Crouse Irving Nursing School in Syracuse. A roommate of hers in Boston, who was also a fellow nurse, was interested in one of my intern mates at HUP. The two women had decided to see the world via its hospitals, and Philadelphia was the next stop. When my friend asked me to join the three of them for dinner, I was available. At the hospital, I was making $100 a month over room and board. Nancy and I soon spent all of my salary on dinner, concerts, and ballgames together.

Nancy was Catholic, and I had grown up in a predominately Protestant town. My Quaker family taught me to respect people of other faiths, yet there seemed to be an exception for Catholics. The justification I recall for this was that the Catholic Church insisted that everyone who married a Catholic become Catholic and raise any children as Catholics. When I had been younger, I'd always agreed that this criticism of the Catholic Church, and its adherents, was justified. But now I had met Nancy.

And to my great pleasure, I found that my mother and father both trusted my judgment in the matter of my falling in love. If they were reserved about my feelings for a Catholic girl, they generally kept it to themselves. Indeed, early on in their own relationship with Nancy, it was clear to her that my parents basically were loving people, and in the end did not really care about the differences in our religions.

In 1965, American culture was beginning to undergo a profound change. The combination of the war in Vietnam and the Civil Rights Movement challenged some of the most rigidly held beliefs of an America still dominated by the generation that had survived World War II. I didn't see myself as an agent or participant in the country's impending transformation. I was in love with Nancy, and I had been drafted. Those were the facts of my life at the time.

I was more impressed with Nancy's close-knit, supportive family than I was deterred by our religious differences. In fact, their values seemed almost identical to my own. I couldn't see why my grandmother had been so afraid of Catholics.

In July, as I was starting my second year in surgery training, and just as our romance was deepening, I received my draft notice, and was ordered by the Iowa draft board to get a physical exam. Passing the exam, I was assigned to the Navy, and sought advice from a former Navy doctor at HUP. He encouraged me to go directly to the Naval Bureau of Medical Personnel, to see what my duty choices were.

Nancy went with me. I was handling the abrupt change of my career plans well enough, probably because there was a great comfort in facing such an unknowable future with a strong partner at my side.

The Commander said he had me penciled in for a ship surgeon position, which meant I would be limited to treating the rare trauma and occasional appendectomy cases each month. Since I had been drafted, and had begun to view my participation in the draft as a way to advance my career, I was looking for a job in which I could advance my surgical skills. Without a second thought, I requested assignment to a war zone hospital. My father had never talked of being exposed to physical danger during World War II, and maybe for this reason I didn't explore the physical risks inherent in going to Vietnam. As with most young men thinking of war, I did not consider the psychological risks either.

In that interval between the draft notice and my reporting to Camp Pendleton on August 8th, 1965, Nancy and I took the train to New York City to see the World's Fair. It was a luminous time, and every problem seemed surmountable. I suffered from what I now realize was the delusion that I was in charge of all the big decisions of my life. In hindsight, the most significant moments—like being drafted or falling in love—were simply coming my way.

Nancy lived with two other nurses in a small apartment six blocks from HUP. I lived in a house-staff dorm in a wing of the hospital. Her evening shift often ended at 11 p.m., and, when I was not on call, I would meet her in the ER and walk her home through the tree-lined University of Pennsylvania campus.

I wanted to be with her every possible moment. Sometimes we went to parties with other couples, but we soon discovered that we did not need an event or outside entertainment; all we wanted was the ease of each other's company. We spent hours talking about childhood memories, family interactions, what seemed like great successes and failures, and how we were dealing with challenges with roommates and co-workers. We had become confidants, and were respectful of each other. Having Nancy in my life made going to war seem a brief detour. I knew that I had to go on this journey to Vietnam, and I was beginning to sense it would be bigger than I could anticipate. But I also knew that Nancy would be with me emotionally. We did not talk or think about marriage at that time; instead we stayed in the cocoon of the present. I was eager to prove myself worthy of this beautiful woman who believed in me.

The last night—before my flight across the country to Camp Pendleton for intensive basic military training—was upon us. Both Nancy and I had work schedules up to the time of my departure, and our friends had planned a party for us. We tried to be gracious to our colleague and host Joanne, who had organized the event that night, but we needed time alone, time the intimacy of which would somehow last for us through the year's separation. Since the South Jersey Shore had been a site of earlier quiet times together, it called to us as a special place that we needed to visit again. We left the party early for the ocean.

It was dark when we reached the shore. As we wandered among the dunes topped with bunch grass, we disturbed flocks of sandpipers with their clear, high calls. The breaking surf reflected the moon's light. We didn't linger long. We just needed to be in the presence of a power as big as what we were feeling. As I felt Nancy shiver next to me, I marveled at the enormity of the night sky, which was un-obscured by city lights. A shooting star briefly flared across an arm of the Milky Way. An owl called, and then swooped over us. I thought of our looming yearlong separation, and somehow knew that we would find each other again. We did not talk about the war zone or my safety. It never occurred to Nancy or me that I might die in Vietnam. Nor did it occur to us what emotional strain the war would inflict upon us.

My printed orders read that I was to report to Station Hospital Da Nang, known as Naval Support Activity (NSA). But first, I was to report on August 8th, 1965 to Camp Pendleton Marine training base. I was to ship out August 24th from San Francisco. Although many thousands of miles were to separate us, I trusted Nancy's love in every respect. Within a month of last seeing one another, our letters began to speak of marriage and a lifetime together.

The training at Camp Pendleton was called "Field Medical Service Training," and was developed for doctors, corpsmen, chaplains, and medical service officers.

Unlike the seventeen- and eighteen-year-old enlisted Marine recruits, this group of drafted men was clearly more mature, and had established some of their own authority in facing the world. They were therefore not as likely as the recruits to take orders easily. In the case of this "Field Medical Service Training," however, there was enough pervasive fear among all of us about where we were going to ensure that we were always on good behavior.

Over the next two and a half weeks, we had the beginning course on how to survive in the field in combat when attached to an infantry battalion. I was, apparently, in better shape than most of my classmates to handle the training. I'd had experience, first, as an Explorer Scout, at age fifteen, when my troop had taken a twenty-day trip in the Boundary Waters of the Superior National Forest of Minnesota, along the Canadian border. The, during the summer between my first and second year of medical school, I had done a survival hike with a Stanford classmate into the Mendocino National Forest, in California. For six days, Tom Skully and I had hiked a rugged thirty-mile loop carrying one pound of oatmeal between us. We ate what we could find, and slept on hard ground. Few of our camps were near water, and edible food was scarce. Hunger had dominated our thinking as we had grown increasingly weaker. Nothing at the Field Medical Service School was as difficult as those earlier two experiences had been, which gave me a false sense of security about what I was to get into in Vietnam.

While at Pendleton, we were given multiple lectures on how to survive on the battlefield. We simulated boarding a landing craft, and the transfer from landing crafts to ships. Daily, we went through obstacle courses for fitness improvement. We crawled under live machine-gun fire, learned how to strip, clean, and fire a .45 caliber handgun, and on one occasion survived a particular chaplain's reckless lack of control of his loaded M1 rifle. No doubt he had never held a loaded gun before, and was used to speaking with his hands, with animation. He swung the muzzle of the M1 in a 360-degree arc, causing the instructor and the class to "hit the deck" (almost the first time I had heard the phrase). We also went on a three-day field exercise, spending one night in a trench and one night on perimeter guard.

The entire course was useful, and the experience of the live machine-gun fire set a tone of reality that would serve me well when I was first fired upon in Vietnam.

Surprising to us, there was no time spent preparing us for the most important task we actually would be performing: how to resuscitate severely wounded men, how to address large wounds surgically, and how to work at times without the equipment we needed. We had assumed that we would experience such things in Vietnam. So, as a consequence of not seeing those details in training, our anxiety grew steadily.

At the completion of that course at Pendleton, we were transferred to Treasure Island in San Francisco, to await our flight to Da Nang. My parents had flown out to be with me for these few days. We toured the Stanford campus and visited San Francisco, but I was so tense and worried, I was not fully present to them. I was beginning to sense the split between the civilian I had been and the wartime man I was to become. I told my parents about my love for Nancy and our thoughts of marriage. If they had any reservations about her Catholicism, they kept it to themselves. My self-doubts about my medical skills preoccupied me so much, I was even beginning to forget what Nancy looked like. I felt alone and unprepared.

CHAPTER V

To the War Zone, Da Nang, September 1965

10 |u|12013

On August 28th, I left northern California on a military plane filled with soldiers, sailors, and Marines in uniform, all strangers to one another, all bound for Vietnam. We had trained at bases across the country, and would be dispersed to units throughout Vietnam that were suffering critical gaps in their rosters. During that flight, we mostly were deep in personal thoughts, and not aware of each other. We refueled in Hawaii (and would again at Midway Island and Okinawa). While in Honolulu, we were taxied to an ancillary terminal, at which there were only military aircraft. We were not allowed off the plane. It seemed as though we were either on so secret a mission that the military didn't want anyone to see us or—more likely—that they didn't want any of us to have second thoughts. Honolulu was, however, a quite appropriate place to have second thoughts, given its remarkable beauty. We had seen it from above. And even from from the airplane parked on the tarmac, we could see palm trees waving in the distance. Through the windows of the nearby civilian airport facilities, we watched seemingly carefree vacationers talking and joking.

But of course I knew that many on the plane with me would not return alive, or would come back injured and maimed. So thinking, I could not look directly at any of my fellow passengers.

We spent two days acclimatizing ourselves to the stunning heat and humidity of the base at Okinawa, while the anti-malaria drugs we had been given reached protective levels in our blood. On the third day there, we boarded the sparse interior of a C-130, where we strapped ourselves into canvas harnesses. Slightly delirious from the heat—and the anticipation—I was relieved that I was finally going. What would the hospital in Da Nang look like? Was it safe? Where was it? How would I find it, and did they know I was coming? From the moment I had begun the journey from San Francisco, I had been waiting to meet someone who might answer some of these questions. I did not realize how quickly, and forcefully, they all would be answered once I got to Da Nang itself.

On the final leg of our flight to Vietnam, we stopped briefly at Clark Air Force base in the Philippines. As the plane banked west over the Bataan Peninsula, I was struck with a sense almost of disbelief. A month earlier, I had walked out of the University of Pennsylvania Hospital in civilian clothes, said goodbye to Nancy, and had gone through the accelerated combat readiness course. Now, looking down on Bataan and recalling its storied wartime history, the 1942 Japanese invasion of the Philippines, the resistance of American and Philippine forces led by General Douglas Macarthur, and the subsequent Bataan Death March, I realized that I was on my way to war. I would soon have my feet on the ground in Vietnam.

Landing at Da Nang Air Base felt like landing on a runway no larger than football field. The airplane at first plunged straight down, hurried into a last-minute nose-up, and landed sharply with a vibrating crescendo as our bodies strained forward against the harnesses. Within minutes of touching down, the humidity and heat had saturated my starched dress khakis with sweat. There was no welcome committee. Everyone on the ground was in a rush, and armed with a weapon. I stood alone for a moment on the tarmac. The airfield was surrounded by rolls of razor wire, and bunkers were placed every 50 yards. One Phantom jet after another, all of them loaded with wing bombs and rockets, roared down the runway, then sharply turned up ninety degrees to avoid what I soon learned was a ground-fire zone. The power and noise of those planes was overwhelming. The ground shook with each passing jet, and for a long moment I was simply bewildered, and remained motionless.

The sun, the heat, the noise and chaos were immediately more than I had anticipated. What had I been thinking when I asked for this assignment? I had been bold and ambitious. I had fallen in love, and now I was off on a journey that promised to give me the solid experience I needed to become a skilled surgeon. Until now, though, the world had seemed more or less rational. It had seemed fair, and in such a world, it had made sense to take risks. But now, standing on that tarmac, I became disturbingly aware that what I had known to be true in Iowa was not going to be true in Vietnam.

But what I had expected no longer mattered at all. I was here. I thought of all the things I knew I could do: I had survived in mountain wildernesses, managed an entire hospital laboratory alone at night, and was able to go into a Wyoming corral to rope a bull and treat its pinkeye. This list did not impress me. In short, I realized that nothing had prepared me for Vietnam. I had been on the ground for just a few minutes, and although I knew nothing about the place, I could already sense—from the noise, the weaponry, the military personnel scurrying about everywhere, the chaos of the place—how little any single individual mattered here.

A passing airman spotted the medical insignia on my lapel and said, "Hey Doc, are you looking for the dispensary?" I didn't know where I was supposed to report in, and replied, "Why not?" I did know that I wanted to get off that chaotic airfield. He pointed more or less into the sun. "It's over there." I went.

The dispensary was not busy, and the staff was sitting about in the waiting room drinking sodas. I introduced myself and mentioned that I needed to find the Naval hospital. Dr. T.J. Rundel, an Air Force flight surgeon, stood up and asked me if I was from Indianola, Iowa. I had not known Dr. Rundel, but now the world had just shrunk! He was from Iowa City, and his brother had recently married an old friend of mine. Out of 20,000 troops on the ground in the Da Nang area, I had just met the one guy who knew me. I was both relieved and startled by the fact that any personage from what already felt like my past life could have found me here.

I would later treat Rundel after he had received minor shrapnel wounds from a mortar attack.

After we exchanged the names of the places and people we knew in common, he directed me to the motor pool, for a ride to the Naval hospital. Neither my driver (a Marine corporal), nor anyone that Rundel asked, seemed to know for sure where the hospital was, only that it was being built near the Marble Mountain helicopter base across the river and five miles south.

The driver told me to throw my duffle in the back and to climb in. He didn't bother trying to reassure me that we would find the hospital somehow, and I didn't ask, for fear that his answer would make me even more nervous. The more people he asked for directions, the more my confidence that we would find the place faded.

The roadside was spotted with old French fortifications: two-story concrete buildings with a bedroom-sized footprint, their walls pockmarked by crater holes from past hostilities. Vietnamese soldiers in green uniforms, carrying guns, were everywhere. I assumed they were not the enemy because they were not shooting at us.

Water buffalos pulled heavy big-wheeled carts. Little children—wearing only shirts—and schoolgirls in long white garments and conical hats slipped through the traffic. Open sewers ran along the streets. The Vietnamese scanned me with sober, wary expressions. The children looked at me, I felt, like scientists studying the results of an experiment. Their expressions were neither hostile nor friendly, and I hoped they knew that I was there to offer my help.

I became acutely aware that how I and the person with whom I was traveling looked could make a critical difference to our personal welfare. The Viet Cong's mission was to kill every U.S. soldier...but who of these were Viet Cong? My uncertainty and the resultant fear started to change me, right away, into a more suspicious person than I had ever been. I hoped that I could be seen as a doctor, and not just another American in uniform. Perhaps then I would be safer.

To reach the still mysteriously located Naval hospital, we had to cross the Da Nang estuary on a ferry crowded with civilians and more gun-carrying Vietnamese soldiers. The bridge that had crossed the tidal estuary a week earlier had been destroyed, some said by Viet Cong, while others thought that it had been wrecked by an over-wide U.S. bulldozer trying to cross the narrow span. My mind swirled with concerns for my personal safety, as the driver kept asking directions to the hospital from passing Americans, who either pointed in vague directions or simply shrugged. There was no sense of coherence. The entire greater Da Nang base was barely five months old and was centered on the Da Nang Airfield, which had been attacked regularly at night in the preceding months. The American units, the Seabee Battalion, hospital units and infantry headquarters battalions were being created around this old and densely populated city. Each unit had to build up its own protective perimeter to defend against the enemy's nighttime incursions.

After crossing the river, we turned south and passed the entry gate to the MAG 16 (Marine Aircraft Wing—Group 16) helicopter base, on the ocean side of the road. The gate for the hospital was further south, and as evening approached, we found it unmanned and barricaded. My driver, planning to return to Da Nang, took one more look south and, by mistake, crossed into a free-fire zone. Instantly, Marines appeared out of nowhere, surrounding us, automatic rifles pointed at us. There was no U.S. presence a hundred yards further to the south of that point. So, to ward off incursions into the area, the territory beyond was subjected to random nightly U.S. artillery fire. By now, it was dark, and we were miles from the motor pool from which we had started. Since all road travel at night was deemed unsafe, we were escorted by Marines to MAG 16 and given cots at the helicopter base.

In the middle of the night, I awoke to the sight of falling parachute flares swaying in the moonless sky, lighting the perimeter and giving a sight line for the Marine outpost that was protecting the base. I had terrible abdominal cramps and had not eaten in hours. I felt I would soon have diarrhea, and could vomit any minute. To reach the four-holer latrine to relieve myself, I would have to cross thirty yards of exposed sand, lit up by the flares, and in my imagination, I envisioned myself in the telescope sights of a Viet Cong sniper. It was a big decision to cross the sand and expose what I now thought of as "my sorry ass," but the need to relieve myself became imperative.

That first night, hunkered down at MAG 16, I realized that the inexperienced driver had put me—and himself—at immense risk when he had driven into the free-fire zone. Had either of us been more experienced, we would have returned to the air base and radioed the hospital that I had arrived and was in Da Nang. I had learned the first, and most important, lesson of many: take charge of your own safety.

In the morning, I found a ride to the Naval hospital and reported to the commander, Dr. Bruce Canaga, an internist who would eventually become the head of the hospital once its construction was completed. At this point, though, one look around the construction site revealed bunkers and footprints of buildings, but no actual functioning hospital. Canaga was living on the construction site with his team of corpsmen, while the Seabees were building the hospital itself. He had received no word from anyone about me. He said that they could use me at C Med for the time being, and offered to drive me there. It was the only functioning hospital in Da Nang, he explained, and ten miles away on the other side of the city.

As we drove, the blast of the Phantom jet fighters made conversation periodically impossible, and served as a constant reminder of the American technical and industrial might in play. Even though the machinery of war now surrounded me, there was comfort in knowing that this escort knew where to go and what to expect. Canaga was about forty-five years old, with graying hair and a long face, furrowed with fatigue. I immediately read him as a kind man. With time, I would learn the depth of his kindness. He would apologize for orders he wished he didn't have to give, and for any assignment he thought might have slighted someone. On this occasion, he must have been aware of my surprise and shock, when I arrived in a war zone, to find no one on the ground aware that I was coming. He had many responsibilities at the construction site, but he had dropped it all to attend to me. I realized later that Canaga's action in calling C Med, and then personally driving me across town, was emblematic of his personal touch and leadership.

The ferry ride this time was less intimidating, and I was getting used to the smell of local food, animal and human waste, and the largely unpaved city of Da Nang. Children defecated and urinated in open ditches. The lack of public health explained the ubiquitous intestinal parasites that I would find in civilian casualities that year.

Canaga and I drove on, passing the area of town called

Dog Patch, a Vietnamese shopping mall that had been thrown together in a month. Dog Patch catered to the nearby Marine outposts with beer, cigarettes, homemade furniture, and numerous "off-limits" establishments. It was a maze of hutches, each built from an assortment of discarded beige packing materials from the millions of pounds of materials sent for the U.S. build-up.

Chickens and pigs surrounded the thatched grass homes, and the practical Iowa boy in me kept looking for family garden plots. But there were no rows of vegetables to be seen. Apparently, the almost constant foreign military presence of the previous eighty or so years—of the French, the Japanese, the French again and now the Americans—had shredded any self-sufficient Vietnamese rural culture.

We continued on, and found the road west of the air base backed up with traffic. Bulldozers were putting in needed culverts and drainage along this century-old roadway that had been built originally, primarily, for ox-carts. The temperature was more than a hundred degrees riding in the open Jeep, and in places there was mud up to the floorboard. We eventually passed a long string of camouflaged trucks hauling Marines and pulling 105 howitzers, clearly heading out to their next skirmish.

CHAPTER VI

C Med, Da Nang, September 1965

10/16/2019

C anaga stopped our jeep in front of the triage tent at C Med, and immediately a Marine corporal shouted at us.

"Move! Move! Move!"

Although Canaga was a Navy captain (equal in rank to a Marine bird colonel), he hadn't realized that we were in the critical space for casualties, between the helicopter pad and the triage door. It was a sacrosanct area.

The man I was to replace was introduced. He gave us a quick, short wave, and hurried off to finish packing, having been tipped off by Canaga's morning phone call that his relief was here. Two months earlier, he had been sent with three days' notice to Da Nang on temporary active duty (TDY), from a comfortable stateside Navy job, leaving his wife and children behind. He was eager now to return home, and didn't wait to brief me. Canaga left me in the triage area, in the hands of a chief petty officer, to return quickly to his construction project. I would not see him again until January, when the Naval hospital opened and I returned there to finish my tour.

Chief Petty Officer Roberts (called "Chief") ran the triage unit at C Med, with a staff of ten corpsmen. Chief was in his mid-forties and had the confidence that came from years of running a stateside hospital emergency room. His shirt

billowed over his generous waist. Round-faced, he had a com-
miserative smile as he listened to my worries about my lack of
experience. When I finally paused, he spoke.

"Look, I have total confidence we can rapidly get you up
to speed. All it takes is your willingness to learn. We'll all be
helping you." He lowered his voice for another thought. "A bigger worry I have with our young doctors is burnout. Don't get
too attached to the individual patients. Just take each one as a
challenge." (I was often reminded of his advice months later,
as it became harder and harder to face a new helicopter load of
wounded men.)

I did not know it in these first days, but my honesty with
him—Chief was someone below me in military rank—and
the corpsmen about my own inexperience was to pay great
dividends. He put mature, seasoned corpsmen with me, every
day, who would give me gentle advice. Something like, "You
might want to give him type-specific blood soon," could save a
Marine's life. These men (the Navy's equivalent to the Army's
enlisted medics) had been working with variously skilled doctors in Da Nang for months. This reversal of roles, with their
advising me on what to do, was practical and necessary in those
first few weeks.

The 3rd Medical Battalion of the 3rd Marine Division had
not been activated during the Korean War. The green tents
we lived and worked in were similar to those used in Korea,
but actually had been last used in World War II in the Pacific
island-hopping fighting of that war. The field hospital at C
Med, which was called a "collecting and clearing company,"
was similar in design to a World War II field hospital. It was
made up of a triage tent next to the helicopter pad, an X-ray
tent, and two air-conditioned and sandbagged operating room
tents. Next to the OR suite were the supply and sterilizer tents
and patient wards. The intensive care unit (ICU) tent was also
air-conditioned, sandbagged, and held twenty beds to be used

for care of the least stable patients. While C Med was designated to hold a total of seventy-five patients, we did not have the staff to handle that volume. Due to that shortage of manpower and space, every day or two we evacuated our post-operative patients to the main air base for the eight-hundred-mile flight to the Philippines or, even further away, to Yokosuka Naval Base in Japan.

After the brief orientation to triage, I walked around the base, to see the layout of the various buildings that were to be my environment, and to locate the tent I would live in for the months until the Naval hospital opened. Each tent on the base held two or three men without crowding, and afforded easy walking room around a central eight-foot pole. My tent had a small label on it in one corner stenciled "Survey 1942." It was old and patched, with a mud floor, and held two cots framed with mosquito netting. It was no doubt the same vintage tent that Dad had used in Europe in 1944. To augment the cots, I went to Dog Patch and purchased tables and chairs made from shipping crates.

Waldron was my assigned tent-mate. At that point, all I knew was that he was an anesthesiologist from Texas. He would become my best friend there. Except for during the rainy weather, Waldron and I routinely kept the tent flaps up for ventilation, since the hundred-degree temperature at night was stifling. Lying on the cot offered a view to the perimeter, beyond which, we knew, was literally an unknown, dangerous world.

Outside the tent was a four-foot deep bunker hole surrounded by sandbags, where I was to spend sleepless nights when we were under attack.

After lunch, I was introduced to our commander, Dr. Almon Wilson, (the chief officer of our 3rd Medical Battalion unit, and a World War II veteran) who sent me to the supply tent to receive proper clothing and gear. Walking there, still dressed in my stateside khakis, I felt that I stood out like a freshman dressed in a college beanie cap. I must have looked out of my comfort zone— clearly just too eager to pick up the helmet, flak jacket, and the .45 handgun—because the supply corporals gave me sullen looks and sent me back for more paper work for the gun. I wondered if I was being yanked around, if they were reveling in their one area of power. Yet perhaps the supply Marines rightly saw the risk inherent in giving any doctor a gun. As I was eventually to learn, they knew that the accidental discharge of a weapon was common for newly arrived M.D.s.

Later in the afternoon, I was introduced to the rest of the doctors at the "club," a roofless patch of ground where one found cases of soda, beer, and gin in iceless coolers. Our unit consisted of three general surgeons (one was Wilson, who now, because of administrative duties, rarely operated), two orthopedists, two anesthesiologists, one internist, one psychiatrist and four GMOs (General Medical Officers, just out of internships). That's what I was…a GMO with only some surgical training and a formal program to go back to after the war. Over the next four months, we added five more physicians to our unit.

A psychiatrist at a front-line unit might seem odd, but it was by no means a luxury. Many Marines who had anxiety attacks could be "talked down" and, with the help of a dry bed and a meal, sent back to their units. Our psychiatrist had his own corpsman, and such occurrences were handled quietly and professionally, attracting little attention. If the anxious Marine had been evacuated out of the country, rehabilitation would have been difficult because he might forever have seen himself as a coward, an idea unacceptable to Marines. Their training attempted to address this possibility. But once in the field, some truly brave men nonetheless found the constant fear and lack of sleep crippling.

Two of the other GMOs and I had been in surgical training when we were drafted, and had arrived in Vietnam with experience of having done appendectomies, hernia repairs, and treating patients with bleeding ulcers, operations always performed under tight supervision. With this background, at first, we were given only as much responsibility at C Med as we could manage. We would assist on patients with multiple injuries, and were in charge of managing the care and resuscitation of those not in the OR. Nonetheless, all of us, no matter how experienced, often found ourselves working at the edge of our competence.

My first night at C Med, I was just finishing supper when the sound of the first helicopter came, followed by another, and another, and another, and another.

The triage tent, set up for twenty stretchers, filled with casualties. The number of stretchers overflowed into an expanded work area between the triage tent and the X-ray tent ten yards away. That night, I was dropped into what felt like a fast-moving river of urgency. It was to go on like this for a year, and was unlike any experience I would ever have for the rest of my life.

I had assumed I would start with a few isolated cases, while teamed up with an experienced surgeon. Instead, the situation was so extreme that I found myself first at one stretcher holding a gushing artery and compressing it while a dressing was applied, then at another station being handed a chest tube while an assistant prepped the chest wall, and yet another station where I took over the central line insertion for rapid blood infusion. The roar of helicopters touching down and the repetitive whump-whump sound seemed to me to be urging us to better control the bleeding, which was almost everywhere. In time, the helicopter's roar was filtered out by some trick of the brain, allowing me to focus on two realities at once: the wounded man in front of me and the unstable status of the many other wounded Marines waiting for an operating table to open.

This big rush of casualties had come from a nearby mortar

attack on the headquarters unit of an infantry battalion, a sup-posedly secure perimeter just like ours at C Med. But the tents had been close together, so that three or four shells had injured many people. The attack killed two men outright. Thirty others were wounded, some with massive internal injuries requiring anesthesia and surgery, and others with shrapnel wounds to arms and legs that were managed with local anesthesia and minor surgery.

After the initial chaos, during which any major bleeding was controlled and airways were secured, Escajeda, the senior surgeon, identified the six most severely wounded, who would be the first to go to the OR. Two men with abdominal wounds and shock went immediately. The other four cases then had to wait several hours for their surgery, and needed fluid replace-ment and pain management until then.

One of my patients had a big chest wound, with parts of ribs and skin missing. We placed a tube in the damaged chest to allow for drainage of fluid and air, and sealed the chest wall hole with a hand-sized layered dressing of Vaseline gauze and several layers of thick padding, all held in place with wide tape in order to make an air-tight seal.

Two chaplains were in triage all evening, quietly reassur-ing the men and, upon request, saying a favorite prayer aloud. For me, their voices gave the busy triage tent a feeling of safe sanctuary.

After an hour, the background noise dropped to just two or three voices moving between each of the thirty stretchers in the expanded triage. We went back over each wounded man, checking on his bleeding and assessing again the urgency for surgery, in order to be sure that we had not missed additional wounds or any other conditions that may have changed.

In the onrush, I forgot entirely about my lack of experience. But after inserting one particularly difficult IV, I had a flash-back to my internship. In my first month of training, I had had trouble starting an IV on a particular patient. To my surprise, five months later, I had encountered the very same woman, who again required an IV. This time, after I had successfully inserted the tube, she remarked, "My doctor, how you have improved!"

Midway through the overflow of wounded that first night, I was able to slow my emotions to a more thoughtful pace. I realized that indeed I could do this work. And I was playing a vital role in the lives of my patients.

It was a matter of staying calm and using common sense. When I had worked as a lab technician in a small hospital for a year during college, I would at times receive multiple stat (urgent) orders. I had learned then to prioritize and to focus one step at a time on the laboratory routine. If I were to let my mind race ahead too much, I would confuse the sequence of tasks that lay before me, an error that would result in wasted time. That learning had been reinforced for me as an intern at the Hospital of the University of Pennsylvania, when I was responsible for thirty patients at night. In those circumstances, the more there had been to do, the calmer I had needed to be. In Vietnam, the need for calm was even greater. There was more pressure, the wounds were massive, the patients often more unstable, and the resources extremely limited.

Fortunately, during the first few weeks, I did not have to make any big decisions, as I would have to do many times later. Decisions such as whether a patient's dire condition would require us to send him to surgery right away, or, if we had time to assess his situation more thoroughly. Would a patient's injuries require us to open his chest immediately in triage? Would he die if we didn't? While no one at C Med wanted me to make a mistake, it was clear to me and the others that I had to improve my skills quickly. There were too many wounded Marines flooding daily into C Med for me to remain on the sidelines.

That first night, after several hours checking X-rays, reexamining wounds, and adjusting IV fluid in triage, I was called to help in the OR, and I needed to scrub. It was the middle of the night. I groped around in darkness until I found the scrub sink door. The set-up was shockingly primitive. A five-gallon water tank with a bottom valve rested on the shelf above the sink. It was easy to turn it on and scrub, but I couldn't figure out how to turn the valve off without contaminating my hands. This not-quite-sterile gap in technique became part of what was called "Da Nang sterile."

As I approached the OR, I noticed that the triage scene outside was one of controlled chaos. But inside the operating room, all was focused and quiet. A few hushed voices around the OR table. I heard the generator grinding, and the air conditioner cycle going on and off, as well as the ever-present howitzer firing from a site a quarter-mile up the road. The only light in the room was the spotlight on the open wound. No outside light entered here, even in daylight. The shadows of the surgeon and corpsmen danced on the shelf-lined wall.

As I approached the table itself for the first time, I could see the problem: to control a bleeding vessel situated at the root of the mesentery, a location where too big a stitch might impair the circulation to the whole small bowel. I jumped in to control the bleeding with my gloved hands, while the primary surgeon placed the stitches, and the corpsman suctioned blood. Visibility and precision were urgently needed. My grip slipped once, and we had to start over again. The patient lost more blood. The operating surgeon recognized the need for a larger exposure to the wound, but while he was extending the incision, the surgical knife blade clicked against shrapnel. Recognizing that sound, the corpsman who was scrub nurse in the operation readied a fresh blade without having to be told to do so. The patient's belly was now open from pubic bone to sternum. That allowed me to get both hands in, and yet to stay out of the way of the critically needed suturing.

There was a run of automatic fire from the perimeter. The thought went through my mind that we could be overrun by Viet Cong. But I didn't have the luxury of entertaining such thoughts for long because the man on the table before us was so critically ill. I was not going to allow my last act on earth to be that of running away, at my patient's expense. I sensed right away that everyone in our tiny tent hospital had the same devotion to the task at hand. It was never verbalized, but it was never doubted.

Hours passed in what seemed like moments. Conversation was sparse, consisting of coded phrases between surgeon and anesthesiologist: "Fresh blood *now!*" "We've got pathologic bleeding." "What's the urine output?" All too often the anesthesiologist tersely demanded that we "just stop the bleeding for a while so I can fill his tank up with blood." There was no light conversation or humorous banter, nor anything else to distract us from the grave situation at hand.

Later that night I briefly looked up from the table when someone had come into the operating room to report on our next patient. My hand must have moved slightly, and in its doing so I lost critical exposure of a bleeding vessel. The surgeon I was helping cursed. "Never take your eyes off the field. Never, never."

To this day, I judge a surgeon by the same standard.

About 4:00 a.m., the cooks sent in word that they had fresh cornbread and milk, and one by one we took a break. It was mid-morning before I could retreat to my tent for a fifteen-minute nap.

Sometime later, I had a chance to write to Nancy and my parents, and I tried to capture the essence of this first night in my letter. I was now less a neophyte than I had been just twelve hours earlier, and I had performed under pressure. My prior training had proven to be better than I had thought, and my instincts had carried me through. I wasn't just relieved; I was excited. I was sure I had found my calling.

I had considered writing a journal, but during my basic training, I had written to Nancy that I would prefer something else: "I may not keep a diary, and will just write you daily." I loved her, and wanted to be in contact with her with as much personal news as possible. Each letter I wrote was an important document to me, almost as important as the daily letter I received from her. Also, after arriving at C Med, I realized that there simply may not be sufficient time to do justice to a daily journal entry as well as a letter to Nancy. On September 8, 1965, the morning after that first night, I only had time to write: "Oh how I would love to be reveling in holding you, but a helicopter just landed, and I have to go." Three days later, I wrote to her, "I am depressed. I am seeing destroyed bodies, sights too awful to even think about."

This was the emotional reality, despite C Med's functioning so well under extraordinarily difficult conditions, and even allowed me to flourish as a surgeon, because of the pervasive spirit of cooperation from everyone. The doctors, dentists, corpsmen, chaplains and the Marines themselves, worked together. The entire unit was free of ego, power moves, and interpersonal bickering. It was clear that everyone just wanted the best for these wounded young men. That was our focus, front and center.

We called the corpsmen at C Med our "sixty-day wonders," sixty days being the length of their formal medical training. They had all started out as Navy recruits who had shown a particular aptitude for medical work, and as a group they were to be among the most highly decorated for their service. Although there were military-service women in Vietnam, there were no women, nor any female or male registered nurses at C Med, or later when I worked at the Naval hospital. The corpsmen's skill strengthened with experience, as ours did, and they became quite competent, no matter whether in ICU, the OR or in field first aid.

In retrospect, I should not have been surprised to find that we were asking corpsmen to do jobs in surgery that many trained nurses were not permitted to do in civilian life. For example, holding a compress to a fractured liver or finishing the skin closure of a belly wound. After all, I had no experience resuscitating major trauma victims up to that point in my own training, and suddenly that was what I was supposed to do. There is no more primal—and brutal—a form of learning than when someone's life is at stake.

The center of my learning experience was in the operating room. The tent itself covered a 16 x 32 foot wooden floor. It was divided into two sections by a partition of canvas, allowing communication between the anesthesiologists at the two operating tables. The canvas was old and moldy, and it leaked. It was no different from the tents in which we lived. The smell in the OR was a unique blend of canvas, anesthesia-gas leaking from the mask, iodine used to prep the surgery site, and the musty odor of fresh blood on the drapes and plywood floor.

This was the inner sanctum at C Med. It was also the bottleneck in the progression of the wounded men's hopes to find their way to safety and home. Only corpsmen who were surgical techs, blood bank personnel, anesthesiologists, surgeons, and surgical assistants were allowed entry to the OR. And no one—no one—went into the OR unless he was needed there.

The only message that ever reached the surgeon at either table was a heads-up on the state of urgency in the line of those patients still needing to get into the OR. The turnover time from commencing one surgery, and then cleaning and preparing the room for the next case, averaged two hours, which was quite efficient given the magnitude of the surgeries involved. Many times, we could have used two or three times the number of ORs and surgeons. In some cases, we were so hopelessly behind that some new but stable casualties had to be sent on the long flight to Clark Air Force Hospital in the Philippines for their surgery.

There was never confusion about the urgency of the surgery. Operations were not elective; there were no written permits, no explanations of what to expect. The wounded Marine was simply told, "You're next." The surgical team was the sole decision-maker, and the outcome depended entirely on us. There was none of the shared responsibility that comes from a patient's (or that patient's family) signing an informed consent, as was required at home. The families were twelve thousand miles away, and had no knowledge of the crisis at hand. We on the medical team were essentially next of kin to these wounded men, and we felt every ounce of that responsibility.

The surgeons I learned from thought out loud, shared their observations, and actively drew the entire team into identifying the issues and priorities for each patient. This was especially true in determining the incision point for the removal of shrapnel. CT scans had not yet been invented, so we had to imagine the internal location of the metal and the extent of the injury. We did so by using the few things that we did have: two-dimensional X-ray films and the location of the entry and exit wounds.

The first part of the operation on a major case involved a delicate balance between stopping rampant bleeding while maintaining adequate blood flow to vital organs like the heart and kidney. The anesthesiologist monitored that balance with tools that are rather crude by current standards: a simple blood pressure cuff, an EKG monitor for the heart, and visual observation of the color of the blood (pale to dark red), which would allow us to assess the amount of oxygen in the blood itself. When the surgeon opened an extremity or belly wound in order to control internal bleeding, the bleeding would actually increase due to the release of the tension on the punctured blood vessels. To close the hole in the bleeding vessel, it was then necessary to clamp temporarily the artery or vein. This would stop the bleeding and allow stitches to be placed, thus closing the puncture site. Everyone had to do his job quickly and with precision.

Days after my arrival, we had another all-night onslaught of constant helicopter traffic, with casualties arriving every five minutes. The night was filled with crescendos of sound from approaching helicopters. We soon had many more patients than doctors. Again I would be rushing from one stretcher to the next, starting IVs, applying pressure dressings to the bleeding sites, and deciding who needed blood and who did not. At some point that night, I made the transition from someone who was following suggestions and taking orders to someone making the decisions and giving the orders. There was no other choice. The people who might tell me what to do were too busy saving someone else's life.

When most of those patients with major injuries had been tended to, I lined up the fifteen men who had injuries that could be managed with local anesthesia, and oversaw the dentists and available corpsmen as they removed dead tissue from the wounds and stitched up bleeding vessels with sutures.

Within weeks, I was doing more complicated procedures than I had previously thought possible. There was no set beginning or end to these days. Sometimes I didn't even know what day it was. The helicopters thudded towards us day and night. We had no regular schedule. I ate when I could and, whenever I could, I slept, collapsing on my bunk. Only mail call provided relief and diversion from operating, eating, sleeping, and operating again. In the fall of 1965 in Vietnam, we had no radio, no newspaper, no music, no baseball scores and certainly no cell phones or internet. Occasionally, I would get a letter from home speaking of topics so remote that they seemed to describe a life that I had never known or would ever know again.

For example, based on our common interest before the war in college football, Nancy had written to me that Stanford had recently beaten Army, 31 to 14, in a football game. I so loved Nancy, but I do remember thinking for a moment to myself, "Who cares?" I also realized in that moment that I had changed, and that although the score of that game was of little importance to me, the cadets who were playing in the game were very important. Graduates from West Point—first lieutenants in combat situations—had an extraordinary mortality rate in Vietnam, and perhaps many of the men in that football game would soon be serving in the Vietnam conflict. Maybe even those cadets were not fully consumed by the outcome of the game because they realized that soon they would be directly involved in war.

I lived not by the time of day, but by the sounds and flight patterns of the helicopters, which often signaled numbers of new bloodied casualties dropping down to us from the sky. I could pick up the sound when it was a half-mile out. It would build to a crescendo, and I would feel the reverberations increasing in my chest until the chopper landed. I wrote to Nancy about those helicopter arrivals: "A helicopter came in at full speed and hit the pad so hard that two wheels were damaged. The door gunner had been hit in the chest."

To this day, almost fifty years later, I am affected by that sound. When I hear it, I jerk my head around instinctively, to locate the helicopter's flight. Without fail, still, when I hear that sound, I feel my throat tighten.

The most urgent flights came in nose tilted down, barely above the treetops, to take advantage of the most efficient aerodynamics. The very sound of those particular flights formed a kind of language of its own, a language we well understood, that usually meant either the patient was in extreme distress or the pilot or crew of the helicopter had been wounded while picking up the casualties.

The choppers carrying the seriously wounded descended faster than the others, and the four corpsmen moving the stretcher to the triage area ran faster. Two helicopters coming in within minutes of each other, or multiple stretchers arriving in the same moment, or the "short leg look" (boots resting too high on the stretcher) which meant land mine injuries, caused everyone to move much more quickly because such an injury meant the risk of exsanguination, which is to say bleeding to death. Often, we would get three or four wounded from the same flight. There was limited advance radio contact, so that we never knew how many to expect.

On September 26, I wrote to Nancy, "In a five-hour span, we had eighteen bad casualties and four DOA. No time will ever compare to these days, for being so essentially needed...I have gotten over the initial horror...The more severe the injury, the more focused I become."

Many times, there were wounded civilians, including children, on the same flight. We usually operated on the children, and when they were stable, we sent them to the civilian hospital. Belly wounds in the Vietnamese would reveal hundreds of roundworms exiting a bowel injury and squirming about in the peritoneal cavity. At other times, there were wounded South Vietnamese soldiers, who would be sent by ambulance to the Vietnamese Army hospital downtown once we had gotten them stabilized.

Rarely, we would receive and treat wounded Viet Cong prisoners, which earned us the wrath of our Marines. There was a recurring rumor that, when they were turned over to the South Vietnamese Army, these Viet Cong would be taken by helicopter and dropped from the air into the night on the way to the referral hospital.

CHAPTER VII

Daily Life at C Med

At C Med, we were living in what was basically a carved-out patch of dirt on a hillside near the city of Da Nang. In quiet moments, we tried to create some sense of routine and normalcy, through games of volleyball and gatherings at the "club." We made an attempt to emotionally decompress.

The eating arrangements for C Med were made in a wood-framed, open canvas tent outfitted with rough tables and benches. The food-line began with a stack of large, compartmentalized tin trays, in which the food looked uniformly like yellow mush. Much of it was canned and had little taste. I complained about it to Nancy: "I would have starved by now without peanut butter and jelly." Such complaining did little to improve the food. But as the year went on—particularly if the weather were good—fresh food did arrive.

C Med was egalitarian and informal about rank, which enabled the whole unit to eat together. After eating, we went through the line to rinse our plates in big garbage buckets full of heated water. Sometimes the last bucket in line remained clean enough to be used for warm evening showers. There were no women on base, and there was no privacy. The shower was a 55-gallon, hand-filled drum, elevated on a platform so that we could stand beneath the contraption. It emptied into a perforated can serving as a shower bib. Except for the occasional dishwasher shower, showers were cold and fast, and the hillside took care of the drain-off.

My needs were simple now, as I wrote in another letter to Nancy: "Three joys: letters, showers, cold beer."

The hospital had its own diesel generator, which powered the X-ray unit, the OR lights and the power lines to each of our tents. The X-ray unit was primitive, requiring developer solution in sequence, and then a period of drying of the film so that it could be read. In central supply, a gas-run autoclave that we called "The Dragon" was used for sterilizing trays of instruments. None of us wanted to open "The Dragon" because it hissed and sputtered steam randomly.

Waldron and I picked up two fans at the Naval hospital, which allowed our clothing to dry in the damp heat, and cooled us off as well. The temperature was usually a hundred to a hundred and ten degrees Fahrenheit, with high humidity. I cut some sleeves and legs off my clothing, and we all wore rubber sandals (called "Ho Chi Minhs") that were made from tires and sold in the Dog Patch mall. I hand-washed my clothing, removing sweat and some dirt, although bloodstains from the OR were more resistant. Soon, all my clothing was permanently stained with other men's blood. Considering our modern awareness of transmission of diseases by contact with infected blood, such as hepatitis C, we were naively careless. We wore no gloves while working in triage, unless we were doing a sterile procedure like a tracheostomy, a cut down, or insertion of a chest tube. Water was delivered every other day in a tank trailer called a "water buffalo," which was parked near the mess tent. We each had a five-gallon container of water for personal use. I shaved in front of a small mirror on a pole outside our tent. The water was so heavily chlorinated that it was disgusting to drink. The Marines added Kool-Aid to make it drinkable, and called it "Jungle Juice."

It was a big event the day we opened the new officer's club (the "O" Club). The structure had a corrugated metal roof and wooden floors…a bit of civilization, I thought. We gathered there in the evenings for beer or martinis, which we garnished with a fig—no olives were available. Here we would talk over cases—a version of the "mortality and morbidity conferences" to which we had grown accustomed in civilian hospitals, where every complication and death was discussed.

We occasionally griped about there not being enough protection around the perimeter. But once, when complaints reached the commanding officer, he gave us a lecture, reminding us that the Navy was not a democracy, and that although he would listen to any medical suggestions, military orders that came from above were not open for debate.

Waldron spent hours distracting us at the O Club with fine stories, one of which was his account of receiving his rush orders for Pendleton, and on to Vietnam. The placement officer in Washington had told him that he needed to get to Camp Pendleton in California in two days. Waldron was a man with his priorities straight. His wife Claudia and their three little children had just been moved to a base in South Carolina, and would now need to move again, to live with Claudia's extended family in Texas, and he was insistent on helping her with the sudden change. He told the placement officer, "Well, I will just go AWOL, because it will take two weeks to get my family relocated to Texas. I know you don't want that to happen— my going AWOL—because I know how much you need me." After a pause, the officer said that Waldron had his two weeks' leave.

Waldron was a favorite of the entire hospital unit because of his dry wit and Will Rogers-like remarks, and because he was such a talented physician. You could depend on him, always, to tell the truth, directly, no matter the situation. He did not place a lot of emphasis on differences in military rank. He never wore his .45 or his commander insignia, to avoid being targeted were we to come under attack, of course. But also he wanted it known that he felt that we were all in this together. A hint to this conviction lay in the fact that, although he was an officer and a physician, he knew the names of every enlisted corpsman with whom we worked.

He and another anesthesiologist would regularly help in the triage tent with the initial resuscitations. They were devoted to the best outcome for each wounded man, and particularly gifted and knowledgeable about resuscitation physiology.

One time they saw us trying to resuscitate a bleeding patient at the bedside, instead of getting him into the OR. "Come on, guys, you can't resuscitate a bleeding patient if you haven't stopped the bleeding first." On another occasion, we were told, "Don't start an IV that leads downstream to an open faucet." This, of course, is common sense when it comes to IV placement, but under tremendous pressure and with someone's life in your hands, common sense can be hard to apply. Or "Look, this is a very bad head trauma case. But at least keep his oxygen up. His blood pressure too." This last was precise and life-saving OR shorthand. We may have done all we could do for the patient's head wound, but if the patient were to lose his airway or had a drop in blood pressure, that too could have a dire effect on his residual brain function.

Waldron and I ascended the living quarters "pecking order" within a month of moving into C Med, and were assigned a tent with a wooden floor, like the O Club. Two sheets of plywood.

On the little makeshift table next to my cot, I had a pile of letters from Nancy and two pictures of her. One was a formal portrait taken at nursing school graduation. Despite our writing of marriage, I still had not made a formal commitment to her. I became acutely aware of my need to be special to her above all others, and for that feeling to be reciprocated. I did not want Nancy dating, but I could not ask that she remain loyal to me without asking her to live the rest of her life with me. We were getting very close to that commitment, doing so by writing to each other daily. We set the groundwork for our marriage by defining in writing what was important to each of us. When she didn't write me daily, I counted the days from one letter to the next. Between her letters, I survived on the very real emotional lifeline of awaiting the next one. When I wrote to her, I tried to give her at least a sense of what I was experiencing. Most of what I was seeing, of course, did not suit a love letter. So I tried to hold onto my memories of her, to remember how beautiful she was, and the wonderful way she treated me. I remembered how, the previous June and July in Philadelphia, when both of us were working long hours, and full of the stress and emotion resulting from taking care of very sick people, we had supported—and comforted—each other. The irony now was that the war and the physical separation were actually increasing our emotional bond.

I tried in my letters home to paint a picture of where I was sitting as I was writing. The hospital was located at the base of an uninhabited hill to the west of us, and the remainder of our perimeter consisted of rice paddies. There were few trees on the hill or in our compound. The main ground cover was a low vine that bore pink flowers, the leaves of which folded like a book when touched. The vines resembled the vetch and the sweet pea that I remembered from roadsides, living in California.

An issue at C Med we had to confront, because of living in tents so close to the ground, was that other animal species naturally lived there with us. One night there was a commotion in the next tent that sounded like hand-to-hand combat, with grunts and thuds. It turned out to be a mortal fight between our neighbor and a rat that had been attracted to the food from a care package the man had received from home. With rats ever-present, we also started seeing more snakes. The most dramatic one was a striped krait, which had been chased from the OR supply tent by a corpsman, and whacked with a bayonet. This particular krait encounter was a one-time event with a species that produces a deadly neurotoxin that is immediately fatal.

But there were other encounters. During one nighttime trip to the triage tent, I almost stepped on an unidentified snake that slithered away into the darkness. Days earlier I had treated a Marine bitten by a green pit viper. The snake had struck his forearm while he had been exploring a tunnel. His arm was swelling rapidly. To treat him, we needed to give him anti-venom, which comes in a solution of horse serum. We gave him a skin test first, and found that he was allergic to horse serum. So we decided that the best avenue was to give him an extremely diluted dose of anti-venom, one part every 15 minutes over a 6-hour period, until he absorbed the whole dose. He tolerated that without reaction. The swelling of his arm did not progress to his shoulder, but there was enough swelling to cause us to make incisions in the skin and fascia of that arm, to release the pressure from the swelling and to prevent impairment of the circulation in the arm. So, although a meeting with a banded krait was considered the worst of all, as we learned, a green pit viper could do serious damage to a Marine as well.

A few months later, I had the opportunity to learn more about these kinds of snakebites. I was given leave to visit Bangkok, Thailand, on Rest and Relaxation (R&R) for a week. I had become a self-appointed snake expert in triage, where, by this time, we had seen several snakebites. I scheduled a day-trip to the Southeast Asia regional resource center for the production of the anti-venoms that we used in the field. I was able to see many types of snakes, including a banded krait. A snake handler was also there that day, holding a six-foot boa constrictor that he would place on a tourist's shoulders for a photo opportunity. The snake farm in Bangkok had become a tourist attraction as well as a pharmaceutical plant.

It was set in a grassy park surrounded by fenced fields. The grassy area was lined with cages for raising rodents (snake food) and with tight glass enclosures for at least fifty varieties of poisonous snakes. Cobras, kraits, and green pit vipers were the main snake threats to Marines in Vietnam. I watched as workers milked venom from open-mouthed snakes. The nearby fields were used as pastures for horses and sheep that would be injected with sub-lethal doses of the milked venom. These animals were actively producing the anti-serum that could then be isolated for neutralizing the toxins in the snake-bit patients. (Thus the term in the treatment: "horse serum.")

The place had some of the feel of my grandmother's farm. My grandmother had no venomous snakes, to be sure. But she had pigs, and there was always the danger of one of her pigs attacking a child, which sometimes happens. So, the verdant pleasures of the two farms—the snakes' and my grandmother's—held possible, and real, dangers.

We learned many subtleties in the treatment of poisonous snakebites during my year in Vietnam. In the typical night time jungle encounter, the snake could rarely be identified, a problem that forced us to use the more problematic polyvalent antisera, rather than the drug that was intended, for example, just for pit vipers alone. The more specific drug carried fewer side effects. The great majority of the cases I treated were presumed to be from green pit vipers, which produce a toxin similar to that of our North American rattlesnake, although less toxic.

One big surprise to me was that so few cases were fatal. Many bites occur without envenomation, and many victims receive only a small dose of poison, causing minimal swelling. This finding—coupled with the dangers of the horse serum, i.e. allergic or anaphylactic shock—meant that we reduced our use of the anti-venom to cases of rapid progressive swelling or systemic symptoms, such as nausea, a drop in blood pressure, general weakness and dark urine.

The countryside and all roads around Da Nang were dangerous, particularly at night, because, under the protection of darkness, the Viet Cong would plant land mines. We had between twenty and thirty Marines on base with us, at all times, who were in charge of our security by guarding the front gate, and by manning the eight bunkers around our perimeter. On most nights, parachute flares lit the area, and howitzers routinely fired at the foot trails that the Viet Cong used for infiltration. Overhead there were tracers from small arms fire. A Marine on our perimeter would periodically fire a burst of rounds at some perceived movement, and then everyone else on the perimeter, nervously thinking they were being fired upon, would in turn also fire. This rhythm of activity, with the sound of small arms firing and the background noise of artillery firing a quarter mile away, filled the air each night, in cycles of intensity.

CHAPTER VIII

Recon Unit, October 1965

10/18/2019

The job of the Marine reconnaissance (Recon) units was to gather information about enemy buildup and movement. They had our greatest respect because of their ability to sustain long-term patrols while evading detection. In the mountainous jungle regions, they would hide in small groups for periods of time, limited only by the weight of the communication radios they carried. They wore no helmets, and were in incredible physical condition. They told remarkable stories about their skill in staying hidden from the enemy. In agricultural areas, they deployed in larger units because they could not conceal themselves as well, and faced more of the probability that they would need to fight their way out.

Their toughness did not protect them from the female anopheles mosquito, which carried the malarial parasite plasmodium. Plasmodium completes its complex life cycle in human liver and blood, resulting in the destruction of red blood cells. Patients with malaria develop periodic high fevers and progressive weakness. In the most severe, untreated cases, patients die of liver and kidney failure. One of my Recon patients had spent two weeks in hiding, reporting movements in North Vietnam. Having forgotten to take his anti-malaria medicine, he had become infected. Any Marine with malaria would eventually have to come off the frontline for medical care, and this man was no exception.

Because of our use of prophylactic oral medicine, malaria never came close in Vietnam to being the problem it was early in World War II on Guadalcanal.

In mid-October, some of the Recon men informed us that more Viet Cong troops had arrived in our area, which made night-attacks more likely. Following the warning, and for another 48 hours, everyone at the hospital wore his helmet and kept his flak jacket close by. All of us in C Med made more sandbags, to pile up next to our tents. As a group, we were not brave fighters, and a small comment from a Recon patrol could easily become a big rumor. Our internist grew so worried by the rumors that he started sleeping in the ICU tent, which was completely sandbagged ten feet high. Later in the year, his worry resulted in a bleeding ulcer.

Marines are always trained to think in terms of how to attack. From fragmented stories that I had heard in triage and post-op recovery, I found that, to avoid getting pinned down in any situation, they would attack as a team of three or four men in a concerted action. For example, if the lead man on a patrol was hit by a sniper or an enemy patrol, the tactic was then to go on the attack, to surround and take out the enemy. No adversary was to get by with "hurting our guys."

Early one morning, three critical cases were brought to us on the same helicopter. The two senior surgeons each took cases to the OR, while I would be in charge of the third casualty until the OR would become available. My patient was gasping for air and in shock, having been hit with shrapnel that had left him with holes in his chest and paralyzed from the waist down. Escajada said, "Okay, Ward-o, this is your case. You're on your own, man." At the time I had just weeks of experience under my belt, but he thought I could step up and do the job. I realized I had to.

I had never before been under such pressure, and said to

myself, *Christ, this man is about to die.* I had to make a series of very quick decisions. I was now the one in charge of this situation, and not just the assistant doing surgical procedures in which someone else would be telling me what to do. This was a whole new level of responsibility. If this man died, it was going to be while under my exclusive care.

Working with my two corpsmen, we first addressed his difficulty in breathing.

Normally, the lung is a big balloon inside a rigid chest wall cavity, with a very small amount of fluid in the space between the two. With penetrating wounds to the chest wall and lung, the small pleural space may fill with blood or air or both, and compress or collapse the lung. The treatment with this particular wound was to place a plastic tube between ribs, into the pleural space, and connect the tubes to a glass jug that had an underwater seal. This would allow the blood and leaking air to escape, in effect a one-way valve, so that the lung could re-expand.

We inserted a chest tube in each side, so that this man's lungs would not collapse. (At this time, incidentally, we had old-fashioned glass rods and rubber tubing to connect to the plastic chest tubes. But in the following few months, we would run so low on the rods, tubing, and jugs that we would turn to Coca Cola bottles and copper tubing substitutes.)

The reason for the paralysis in this patient's legs was made clear to us in the X-rays. There was shrapnel near his T12 (twelfth thoracic vertebra), and other shrapnel near his spleen. There could be either a direct injury to the spinal cord, or bone and blood compressing the cord. No one in Da Nang at that time was trained to operate on the spinal cord. A neurosurgeon would not arrive in the area until November. Even if there had been a neurosurgeon present, the spinal surgery would have had to wait until the patient's other life-threatening injuries were stabilized.

Although his blood pressure was at 90, the patient soon stopped speaking and became unresponsive. We quickly placed a tube in his trachea for ventilation, and were pumping in more blood when he stopped breathing altogether. One of the corpsmen continued the ventilation for the patient for several hours, until we could take him to the OR. His urine output remained low, as did his blood pressure. He required continual blood transfusions. His belly grew bigger. Given this, and the location of shrapnel near his spleen, it was obvious that we needed to explore his abdomen.

When Escajeda was finished with his first case, I accompanied my patient to the OR and, under Escajeda's guidance, removed the damaged, bleeding spleen. This was the first splenectomy that I ever performed. Escajeda took over dealing with the bleeding liver. Both the spleen and the liver are so soft that bleeding is hard to control by the usual means of stitching and clamping vessels, and then ligating the bleeders. While his injured spleen was now removed, the patient's blood pressure was now in the mid-70s, and the bleeding in the liver was not yet controlled. It occurred to me then—abruptly—that this man would likely die on the table. I felt weak-kneed, but within seconds was able to fight my way back to the present moment and the task at hand.

We placed multiple washcloth-sized "lap pads" between the liver and the diaphragm, and more of them between the liver and the intestine. Our sewing up the abdomen succeeded in cinching the pressure on the liver, and stopped the bleeding. We removed the packs the next day.

The procedure worked, and the patient was evacuated to Clark Air Force Base a day later. He would be paraplegic for the rest of his life...but he would have his life.

As for me, I had thrown my entire heart and newfound skills into this young man, who had been so close to dying, yet now he would live. I felt empowered, and finally relieved of the tension I had been holding inside for weeks. For one, I hadn't become distracted during the procedure by worry about his paralysis. I had known that I could do nothing about it, and that it would have to be addressed later. At age twenty-seven, I had led a team in an unexpected "save." It was a profound experience for me.

As I watched that Marine being transferred onto the evacuation flight, Escajeda gave me a pat on the back. "Come on, we have more cases to do," he said. I realized that now I was trusted. I knew that I could have done everything perfectly, and still have lost that Marine. Indeed, that was exactly to be the outcome many times in the coming year. But this was my first time in charge of a case, and it gave me great confidence to have pushed beyond the limits that, before, I had perceived in myself.

One of the great gifts of the intensity of that year was that I learned to focus on what I was doing for extended periods of time. There was no ambiguity about what we were to do at each moment. At C Med, any personal wishes or other needs were subordinate to that.

But I wanted such certainty in all aspects of my life, both inside and outside medicine. I knew I had Nancy's solid support, as well as that of my parents, my doctor friends and the whole team of corpsmen. At night, nearly everyone in C Med would settle into writing...letters home, diaries, journals. Writing helped me to formalize the learning moments in each day, and was forcing me to be introspective about life itself.

No doubt, in the process of putting my thoughts on paper, I was discovering myself as much as I was discovering Nancy. For example, on October 30, 1965, I wrote to her, "Bad night. Sixteen dead and thirty-three wounded. Very close to us. Had to keep helmets and flak jackets close by while in triage." In the process of writing back and forth, Nancy was also discovering things about me, and wrote to me, "I'm sorry last Friday was such a bad day, with all the casualties—you deserve to be discouraged and depressed, if anybody does."

Our connection could not have been stronger, even had we been together every day. In my letters to her, I spoke about the teamwork and the way in which the people around me somehow maintained composure in the midst of the noise and chaos and urgency. Although Nancy, as an emergency room nurse in Philadelphia, and Dad, as a doctor during World War II, knew about medicine and surgery, I still felt I could not adequately speak about, nor capture, the horror of some of the destroyed bodies I had seen. So often I didn't try.

During this time, I was also reexamining my basic beliefs about the world and my relationship to my fellow man. I had grown up in a protected home, part of a small-town community where there was no contact with the real hardship that I was to see in Vietnam, and I had believed that my success so far had been based on sheer hard work and on my own personal focus. But I'd never personally confronted the kind of desperation and struggle that I saw people—and I mean here the Vietnamese people—encounter in Vietnam: they faced war, occupation, death, the death of their families, intermittent homelessness, poverty, parasitic infestations, and inadequate education. In Vietnam, I felt submerged in the suffering of others, and I felt it personally.

And of course, I always thought about what would happen to these young Marines that we sent home without legs or arms, or without full brain function. From this experience, I slowly underwent an enormous change in my thinking. I now felt that I inhabited the real world, a world that wasn't always fair or controllable, that was full of heartbreak and loss. I learned that success often depended on a team, not just a single individual. What I could do here was to ease the medical conditions that were part of the complex, even monumental, burden that was being borne by all these victims of war.

I also had another job. While my time was often overwhelmed by the injuries I was treating in C Med, I was also helping to run the medical clinic for the 30,000 Marines in the greater Da Nang area. Initially we had run the clinic in the triage tent at C Med each morning. But as the troop numbers expanded in the fall of 1965, we needed to move the clinic to separate quarters, where we would see patients up to six hours a day.

The Marine clinic handled all non-trauma medical issues: smaller wounds of the extremities, immersion foot, dehydration, diarrhea, tropical illnesses, and venereal diseases (now called Sexually Transmitted Diseases). On rainy or windy days, when the clinic's tent sides were down, the pungent ripe-cheese smell of the canvas was headache producing. Benches for those waiting for clinic had been set up in a line, and overlooked the flow of incoming casualties with dire wounds. This was no doubt a sobering sight for those men awaiting entry to the clinic for their problems.

Our one internist and the GMOs staffed the clinic. When new casualties would arrive in triage, we would close the clinic down, and the patients would be told to come back the next day, unless they were seriously ill and needed admission. The lineup for treatment was always long, but had little of the drama and urgency of the triage tent.

The clinic lines reminded me of watching my dad working in his office with a long line of his own patients. He took each patient's concerns seriously, and made each one feel listened to. Recalling that, I worked at being that kind of doctor, here at this clinic. We were, to be sure, dealing with Marines, and my experiences with them were somewhat different, I'm certain, than those my father had with his patients in Indianola. As I wrote to Nancy about two of my clinic patients, "I am afraid the Marine language is contagious. I asked a man in sick call what his problem was. He answered, 'My eye is all fucked up, sir.'... Another Marine, speaking of shrapnel that hit him close to an eye, said, 'But it didn't enter the brain housing mechanism, right, Doc?'"

My clinic duty was not easy. It often came on the heels of long hours of trauma surgery, and I was often quite exhausted. The corpsmen did a stellar job of choosing the patients that we needed to focus on first, such as those with belly pain, in which appendicitis could be a possibility. We treated many infected extremity wounds that came from a Marine's thrashing through the brush, wounds that would only get worse without rest and antibiotics. It was impossible for these men to stay clean while on patrol, and often, with infection, their wounds would grow larger and worse.

In 1965, our list of drugs was surprisingly short and simple: penicillin, streptomycin, sulfa, tetracycline, morphine, codeine, deworming pills, and malaria pills. Sunlight and soap and water were prescribed for open sores and skin rash.

Occasionally within the daily clinic line-ups, we would encounter a Marine just two weeks or so from his arrival in-country, who suffered from dehydration and salt depletion. A Marine in the field routinely carried fifty to eighty pound loads, in one-hundred degree temperatures. These men would be out on continuous patrols through deep mud and intractable jungle, often for many days. While on patrol each night, they would dig a new trench for protection, and then would stand guard half that night. New men needed several weeks to acclimate themselves and to learn how to handle the stress, as well as to understand that they would have to keep going even when they were exhausted. Because of their youth and, in many cases, athleticism, they usually succeeded.

Nonetheless, a simple cluster of symptoms like fever, headache, and malaise in Vietnam was much more challenging than would have been the case back home, because of the array of unfamiliar tropical diseases, such as dengue fever, malaria, encephalitis, and meningitis. All these were possibilities for these men, as well as the more common viral flu, heat prostration, or the early phase of gastroenteritis.

After a few weeks in the medical clinic, I was confronted by how little I knew about these exotic diseases. So I signed up for a correspondence course on tropical medicine, which gave me access to the resource books we lacked in clinic. We gradually organized a diagnostic lab, with such basic equipment as a microscope, a tool that we had not been using prior to this. We found a corpsman assigned to our unit who had experience in a lab, who could evaluate blood smears for malaria and stool specimens for parasites. However limited our knowledge, and how minimally equipped the laboratory, we had to make presumptive diagnoses and educated guesses at the best possible therapy.

Treatment of malaria was the dominant focus for our internist. Mild cases presented pink-colored urine, resulting from limited destruction of red blood cells and the subsequent appearance of hemoglobin in the urine. Saline infusion is the treatment for massive red-cell breakdown. The sickest malaria patients go into coma because of the effect the disease has on the small blood vessels in the brain. In our clinic, such patients were sent to ICU.

In spite of the consequences, the men were not always diligent in taking their prophylactic medicine. It was hard to convince some of them that they indeed had to fear microbes as much as bullets and shrapnel. But that was the case, and failure to take medication undoubtedly resulted in the deaths of some.

In the clinic, we also came across cases that were unexpected by us, such things as Hodgkins lymphoma with a neck mass and Guillain-Barré syndrome, a disorder in which the body's immune system attacks part of the peripheral nervous system. These gave me the opportunity to write to my father, who understood such conditions better than I did, to seek his advice.

Venereal disease was another common, though less deadly, ailment that we came across in the clinic. It was both painful and embarrassing, and the men would become very anxious and distressed when describing their symptoms. The combination of a high level of testosterone in a male eighteen-year-old's brain, the talk of sexual exploits, and the real possibility of dying soon all conspired to make sexually transmitted disease a common problem. It became, therefore, an essential subject for conversation in every interview that we had with a clinic patient.

I listened to their distress and took their concerns seriously. I learned that some of those who showed up for clinic were worried about something quite different than their stated complaint. One eighteen-year-old Marine, a young man named Tom, whose referral slip read, "urinary tract infection," came from a small town in South Dakota. To break the ice, I talked about my mother's mother, who had grown up shoeless in a sod hut on a homestead there. I had loved her stories of the blizzard of 1888, and how she was denied the only doll in a care-package from Iowa because "the doll was for the poor people, and we had so much more than the poor had." After comparing notes about how my grandmother lived and how Tom had seen remnants of such living quarters—in which the only thing still standing was the wooden door frame—I eased into what I had perceived as the real, and loaded, topic of our conversation.

"First of all, it is very unusual for a young male to develop a bladder infection that is not caused by a bladder stone or a congenital malformation. Both of those seem unlikely in your case, and it is common for young men to contract gonorrhea, which has some of the same symptoms. But the treatment of the two conditions, gonorrhea and a urinary tract infection, are very different. I think you had better give me the unvarnished truth, so we can send you home as healthy as you were when you left."

Tom hung his head, held his breath for a long moment, and then poured out his story. After being on patrol and in constant danger for three weeks, his platoon had returned to headquarters near a village about 30 kilometers from Da Nang. Upon their arrival, he and his buddies received a much-needed pass. They all headed into the nearby town and straight to Madame Nom's, where they could sit around and have beers, and then wander off with one of the girls.

Tom was attracted to a particular girl, and always waited for her. During his first visit to Madame Nom's, he had shown her a picture of his girlfriend in South Dakota. Tom and the girl got into the routine of resting close to each other, listening to music, and she would rub his neck where the machine-gun strap had produced a chromic muscle cramp. He never took condoms with him because he was so sure he would be faithful to his girlfriend. Tom made one particular trip to town, though, in a period of significant emotional distress because of the death of a fellow Marine in the field. Tom poured out his feelings to this woman, whom he barely knew, and with whom he had so little in common (although she certainly had her own trauma and loss). She had comforted him…and within a week of his last visit with her, he suffered a urethral discharge and painful urination.

He made up a story for the corpsman of his unit, of a leech on his penis. The corpsman immediately saw through the hoax, and came up with the face-saving diagnosis of urinary tract infection. I assured Tom that his infection would be cured with penicillin, prescribed it for him and sent him back to his unit. Several months later, I was to treat him for a minor shrapnel wound. When I asked about his girlfriend, his smile displayed a mixture of recognition and embarrassment.

Another common ailment that we treated in clinic was immersion foot syndrome. Immersion foot is a painful, debilitating injury to the skin of the foot, from prolonged exposure to wet conditions. The foot becomes pale, wrinkled and very sensitive, then reddens and becomes quite swollen. Eventually it ulcerates, with a loss of tissue, and there is enough pain when walking that, with this condition, a soldier is not able to go on patrol.

Immersion foot was a great drain on manpower throughout the war, and was often a point of the conversations we had with General Lewis Walt, during his weekly visit to C Med. The general was the commander of the 3rd Marine Amphibious Force and the 3rd Marine Division in Vietnam, of which we were a part. He was the kind of leader who worried about the details that took his fighting men out of action. "Trench foot" had been the name of the same condition during World War II and Korea, where its onset had been more rapid due to colder temperatures. In Vietnam, immersion foot was treated with daily care with dry socks and new boots developed for Vietnam that drained and dried out faster than had the old leather boots.

After witnessing these various conditions in clinic, my parting words to each patient included more than the typical instructions about condoms and venereal diseases. I also always instructed the Marine to be aware of dehydration, to drink extra water, to be smart about the source of that water, to routinely take his salt tablets and malaria pills, and to wear clean, dry socks every day.

I myself suffered to a degree from immersion foot syndrome. On October 6, 1965, I wrote to Nancy with a request: "Could you send me sandals? My feet are rotting," and in another letter: "The rain is heavy and I get soaked in spite of a poncho. The mud is unbearable." A few weeks later, I did receive a pair of sandals from Nancy, which I truly appreciated. The trouble was, they were made of leather, which meant that they would quickly deteriorate in the Vietnam wet and heat. The only sandals that really worked out there were the good old rubber "Ho Chi Minhs."

CHAPTER IX

China Beach

One particularly hot and humid day, after what seemed to us like endless days of heavy casualties, Commander Wilson surprised us with permission for three doctors and three corpsmen to leave the hospital for a swim at the South China Beach. C Med was on the inland side of the city of Da Nang, and the swimming area at China Beach was on the coastal margin of the helicopter base across town from us. It was near the place where I'd spent my memorable—and potentially dangerous—first night in Vietnam, looking for the Naval hospital. Both were close to the construction site of the new hospital, which was still being built by Seabees.

The one-hour trip to the beach took us along a road crowded with farmers carrying heavy loads and carts pulled by oxen. The trip was both scenic and tense, because again we were never certain who might be Viet Cong. Just as we were about to leave C Med, we heard that two young Vietnamese girls had been accidentally and fatally crushed at the area dump by an American truck hauling trash. With this in mind, we all stood waiting for our ride in silence. It was neither the first time we felt guilt by association for the deaths of innocent civilians, nor the first time such deaths reminded us of the tragic reality of this war.

I needed to see something besides the patch of earth on

which C Med was located and the shredded bodies of wounded men that passed through our facility. We boarded the ambulance and headed to China Beach. Once there, we stripped down to our shorts and walked out onto the barren sand. The surf was up and pounding, and proved too rough for our plans to go swimming. No other bathers were in sight. Just ten feet above us, on the landward sand dunes, we could see one of the Marine machine gun outposts of the nearby Mag 16 helicopter base. Not being able to swim was a depressing letdown for all of us. Absurdly, I think we had expected a crowd of happy people—and maybe even girls in swimsuits—but the scene was far from idyllic. We were alone, the six of us, with roiling ocean surf and, we suspected, poisonous sea snakes to one side, and a machine gun and open, exposed beach to the other.

The idea of a swimming trip had captured our minds partly because we were so confined at C Med. I had been there six weeks without leaving the perimeter of the hospital grounds, except for the short trip to Dog Patch for furniture for our tent. We were working long hours under great pressure surrounded by armed guards. I had a picture in my locker of Nancy and me with another couple on the South Jersey shore...another beach on another ocean half way around the world. Unlike in New Jersey, though, China Beach had no concessions—no ice cream, no hamburgers, no suntan lotion—and no other people. We could see just empty miles of unfriendly ocean. It occurred to me that it was more fun being useful at the hospital, although I was already starting to dread the drive back. The looks we had gotten from the Vietnamese on the way over had been most unwelcoming.

I did not go to China Beach again that year. I heard of occasional trips there by others as the year went on, but the place never gained a foothold with any of our people as a popular place for an outing.

Not long after we returned from the beach, a helicopter's

nearby crash-landing brought us quickly to the urgency of the next case. We rushed to the triage tent, where we found a Marine shot through his jaw and neck. My job was to insert an endotracheal tube to protect his airway. He coughed blood everywhere. He was frantic. He could not speak, nor could he lie on his back for long because blood would flow into the hole in his trachea, and nearly drown him. Unsure of what was happening to him, he thrashed his arms around, which kept us from inserting an IV line through which to inject a sedative. He acted like a trapped, powerful animal, forcing us to pin his arms to his sides to somehow get the tube in, and to squirt Xylocaine down the tube in order to numb his cough reflex. My glasses were bloody and opaque. I had to work by feel, my left finger finding the hole in the trachea, and then inserting the tube. As soon as I got the tube in, he was taken to the OR and put to sleep. His bleeding was controlled.

His wounds could have been caused by shrapnel from booby-trap shells, by mortar fire, or by hand grenades, which produce low-velocity wounds that are very destructive, but not as often fatal as bullets. Although wounds from shrapnel can be lethal if a fragment hits a critical part of the anatomy, I had begun to think of the low-velocity wounds as "lucky" ones. High-speed bullets can cause damage well beyond the bullet track because of collateral shockwaves. All missiles (bullets, wood, and chunks of metal) tear holes in human tissue, but often the higher velocity rounds from a gun tumble and, in the same moment, lose their kinetic energy, which is transferred to a kind of sheering force that tears open a wide and ragged swath of tissue. The Marine with the jaw wound was disfigured, but the shrapnel had missed adjacent arteries. A high-speed rifle round to the same location would have ripped blood vessels apart in his neck and probably severely damaged his spinal cord as well.

The next day a truck hit a land mine, turning the cab into a flaming oven. The two men in the cab had only minor penetrating injuries, but in both cases deep and extensive burn injury to the skin and airway. They were anesthetized quickly, breathing tubes inserted before their airways could swell shut, and long cuts were made the length of the thickened and hardened burn scars to allow for expansion of the internal swelling that would occur from the burn. They were given an intravenous fluid formula that had been developed in the previous few years at the Brook Army Burn Center in San Antonio, Texas. Major burn injuries had become specialized trauma cases requiring experience in skin grafting and prevention of burn-wound infection. These men received special evacuation designations, and specialized teams were flown directly from Texas to meet them in Da Nang, and to fly with them back to the Army Burn Center.

Far too frequently, it was the corpsmen attached to the infantry patrols that were wounded with high-speed rifle rounds, while crawling to rescue wounded comrades pinned down by sniper fire. On one occasion, two corpsmen with head wounds were admitted at the same time, and we had no neurosurgeon on staff. Both men had been crawling to the same wounded man. The first corpsman's condition was deemed fatal due to the large amount of brain damage he had suffered, although he was spontaneously breathing. The other corpsman required some cranial bone removal and bleeding control before we could set up a special evacuation to a neurosurgeon located three hours away in Saigon. I don't know what happened to that patient, but I did know that the time it would take before the neurosurgeon in Saigon could operate likely would lead to a fatal swelling of the brain.

We desperately needed a neurosurgeon...but also more doctors in general, more supplies and better equipment. When interviewed after the war, our commanding officer, Wilson, spoke about how heartbreaking those early months at C Med were, particularly when the wounded suffered from the lack of what was commonly available in the United States.

In time, I was given increasing responsibility for some of the sickest and most challenging cases in triage. I hardly noticed the passage of time, overwhelmed as I was by the intensity of both the volume of work and the magnitude of the injuries. A typical case was one we received in mid-October, a Marine who had stepped on a land mine and suffered from wounds to his leg, shoulder, elbow, wrist and hand, as well as a "sucking" chest wound, (a hole in the chest wall so large that with each breath, air comes in and out of the chest hole instead of through the mouth and nose). This kind of wound is often fatal if the hole is not occluded quickly. We needed to insert chest tubes as quickly as possible. As soon as the chest tubes were in, we drained the volume equivalent of one half of the patient's total blood volume.

Both operating rooms were busy in that moment, both general surgeons operating. So I was on my own with two corpsmen and this severely wounded man. In spite of ongoing blood transfusion, his blood pressure was dangerously low. Due to the combination of blood loss and the period of ineffective respiration, he stopped breathing, and we immediately intubated him, and then ventilated him with oxygen from a hand-squeezed ventilation bag. He had so many extremity injuries that it was hard for me to find IV access. He reminded me of a piece of sackcloth with many rips in it. He was leaking from several places, and I feared we would not be able to find a way to put necessary fluids into his body at all.

I tried a new procedure for IV insertion: using deep major vessels for the IV, and placing one catheter in the femoral vein in his groin and another in the subclavian vein, below the clavicle. Both catheters were then threaded into the vena cava for rapid infusion of a large volume of saline and blood. We did not have the time for a thorough cross-match of his blood, and just matched the donor blood to his basic type.

Fortunately the bleeding from his chest injury stopped. Next we explored all his wounded extremities, and removed dead muscle and bone fragments from each one. We found no major injuries to nerves or blood vessels. He later showed signs that his kidneys were injured, and we thought he might need temporary renal dialysis. But we did not have that capacity in Da Nang. So, thirty-six hours later, the patient was evacuated to Clark Air Force Hospital in the Philippines.

Once again, we had done the best we could to cobble a man's body back together. But without knowing the outcome of his case, we simply couldn't know the final story of his recovery. I am sure that some men that we saved in the short run died within days or weeks of leaving us, given the magnitude of their injuries.

But when we could gather outcome information from the hospital in the Philippines, we were able to improve our procedures. One example was the change we made in the treatment of a patient who would arrive at C Med with multiple wound holes in the abdomen. When I had first arrived, the standard treatment had been to search for each hole in the small intestine, and to suture each one individually. From Clark, we received the feedback information that many of these cases had later had leaks of gastro-intestinal contents into the abdominal cavity, from failed wound healing, a situation that brought on peritonitis. As a result, we then began to remove that riddled section of the intestine altogether, instead of stitching the individual holes. The more aggressive procedure brought us greater long-term success.

Later in October, the monsoon season began. We had inches of rain each day. It felt as though the jungle, which had tolerated us up to a certain point, had finally decided to flush us into the South China Sea. Our hospital was situated at the base of a hill and on a gentle slope, so Waldron and I at least were able to make a trench around our tent that, along with our newly acquired plywood floor, kept bare feet and cots from sinking into the mud.

But with the monsoon, there was another danger. Rain put the Viet Cong on more of an even footing against U.S. mechanical superiority. With decreased visibility, our air support was severely hampered, and our helicopters were unable to bring in reinforcements or evacuate the wounded. The long period of torrential rain during the monsoon slowed the gunfire, but actually exacerbated the rate of blunt-trauma accidents.

During one three-day rain, for example, the truck being driven by one of our Marines slid into a ditch, an accident that gave his passenger a depressed skull fracture. The fracture was producing pressure on the patient's brain that needed to be relieved. Escajeda called me and said, "You should know how to do this, Ward-o, and you may never get the opportunity in your training when you get back." Together we drilled holes near the caved-in part of the skull, much as a carpenter would do, and as ancient Egyptians had done centuries before. We used a small instrument, named after the famous neurosurgeon Dr. Harvey Cushing, to pop the depressed bone off the brain and thus relieve the pressure.

As the rain continued falling, the casualty rate generally slowed. The free time that resulted allowed Nancy and me, through our daily letters, to work out how we would negotiate our religious differences. I had told my parents of our plans to get married, and still could read between the lines of their letters that they thought maybe we were rushing this decision. In fact we could not have been more deliberate and thorough in that process. I had written to Nancy on August 16, just eight days after we had said good-bye to each other in the United States: "I told my parents we were in love and talking about marriage." I felt that I understood my parents' reservations, but a larger issue was driving my heart: "Religion is irrelevant.

Let's get married two months after I get back."

I assured my parents that I heard their concern, but that I also knew that they would come to love Nancy as much as I did. I sensed that Nancy's parents, too, might have similar concerns, over their daughter's marrying a non-Catholic, and wrote to her on October 4, about that as well: "Please tell your parents we are getting married soon after I return. Mrs. Trueblood, do you agree? How soon do we have children?"

I thought that some sort of clear declaration of my actual religious beliefs was necessary, so that Nancy would know precisely where I stood. So the very next day, I wrote to her: "My religion is very simple. The need to live a good and productive life that is not driven by fear or a promise, but from my heart.... I can't tell you enough, how lucky I feel to have you in my life."

Nancy, too, was sensitive to the concerns of my parents, and wrote to my mother and dad in October: "Ward is a more mature man than the one I remember who left in August." My mother then wrote to Nancy's mother and mentioned how delightful Nancy's letter was: "We are eager to know Nancy better, and hope to make her feel most welcome in our family."

In the midst of a daily life reduced to mud and steady work around the clock, Waldron and I were invited to visit the chief of surgery, Dr. William Adams, a Navy Captain, at the now partially constructed Naval hospital. Adams had a dry office in a large white building called "The White Elephant" in downtown Da Nang, at Navy headquarters. He had magazines, including the current issue of *Time* that featured an aerial view of Da Nang itself. I remember thinking, "Wow, the Viet Cong probably brought a copy off the rack in Saigon, and are using it to plan upcoming attacks now." We dined at a Vietnamese restaurant downtown that night, and felt quite conspicuous in our uniforms, as we sat among the sophisticated Vietnamese civilians who were also dining there. Until that day, I had assumed that everyone in Vietnam was living as primitively as we were at C Med. But here, the tables were covered with tablecloths and napkins, the first we had seen since we had left the States, and we were served a delicacy, bird's nest soup. I ate it with trepidation while wondering if such a recipe explained the sparse bird life in Da Nang.

Over dinner, we talked about our various backgrounds. Adams was a slight, dignified, and reserved man, and had just arrived from the States. I noticed right away that he was most talkative when describing his military experiences and, especially, his interest in the cardiovascular response to massive blood loss. He had served as a surgeon in the Korean War, and we had a lively conversation comparing the differences in war surgery between then and now. In Korea, he had seen the very first use of helicopters to transport injured men to surgery, and had experience with the resuscitation methods that were used then and, indeed, had been in use even during World War II.

Because Waldron had only recently completed his anesthesia residency in a nationally regarded training program in Dallas, Texas, he was familiar with the latest in physiology research. While Adams had seen many men die of renal failure caused by the lack of timely blood and fluid replacement, renal failure was very rare now in Vietnam because we had both aggressive IV fluid infusion and faster and more agile helicopters that could deliver the wounded from the firefight to C Med within an hour. The average evacuation time in Korea had been three and a half hours. The difference between the one-hour flight in Vietnam and the three-hour flight in Korea was enormous in terms of survival in the Vietnam conflict.

I was later to learn of a personal connection between Adams and Escajeda. Escajeda had been a chief resident under Adams, capping his surgical training at the San Diego Naval Hospital. Later, when Escajeda was the only surgeon to land with the Marine force at Chu Lai in March 1965, he was notified that his youngest son, still a child, had been critically injured in a fall while playing on a rocky outcropping at Camp Pendleton. The Red Cross radioed a message to Escajeda describing the severe nature of his son's injuries, with a request that Escajeda return home. The Navy denied the Red Cross request, explaining that Escajeda was the only surgeon on the ground in Chu Lai at the time, and could not be spared.

Escajeda later received another radio message, this time directly from Adams. Adams had personally performed the necessary surgery on the boy's liver and removed a ruptured spleen. Escajeda's son survived. I eventually heard this story, but not from Adams himself. The conversation Adams always wanted to have with us was focused on how we could save more lives.

CHAPTER X

Politics Meets Reality

A s I've mentioned, the commander in charge of all the forces in the I Corps area was General Lewis Walt, who made many trips to our hospital. He was fifty-three years old, the oldest officer in the field. He was quite tall and had the strong build of a football player. While the formality of saluting was normally abandoned in the combat zone, Walt had such a presence that everyone tended to salute him, except the doctors, who were generally protocol inept. Walt made our encounters less awkward by extending his hand right away, taking off his Marine hat, and asking a question before we could remember how to address him properly. His focus was only on what his troops in the hospital needed. His style was to gather information rather than to try to show his command and power. His clothing, like ours, looked lived in, and sagged from sweat. His care for the men in his command in World War II and Korea was legendary.

Because C Med was near Marine Corps headquarters, we were frequently on the "dignitary tour." Every two or three days, a visiting politician, demonstrating to his voters that he was checking on the war, came to us on a fact-finding mission. I remember these politicians being told by Marine colonels that the U.S. could win the war if they would just send more troops. I wondered how they expected to learn anything about the success or failure of the "search and destroy" tactic—or the war in general—in just the two days of a superficial and controlled visit. Even if I had been given the opportunity to speak of my concerns about the war, I probably would have refrained, for I had only vague knowledge of what was happening beyond our perimeter. I did have a sense that the war was not going well. But I could not be objective, for I was too close to the daily sacrifice, and held too much hope for a good outcome. I felt that anything I might say would simply invalidate the sum of the individual heroic efforts that I witnessed every day.

The congressmen paraded through our intensive care unit tent, by necessity, in single file because of the close quarters. The ICU tent was a dark, windowless, double-length tent surrounded by eight-foot high walls of sandbags. Inside, 20 beds were lined up perpendicular to the center aisle. Since we evacuated the stabilized casualties every day or two, the wounded that the dignitaries saw were always fresh out of the OR, and therefore sedated, stunned, and often incoherently moaning. Many of the wounded had not yet been told of the extent of their injuries, or whether their buddies had survived. The odor of sweat, urine, bile, and disinfectant would have been overwhelming to someone who wasn't used to it. It did look similar to what some of these dignitaries—if they'd had military experience—may have seen in Korea or World War II. Most of them, though, were speechless; some even appearing on the verge of passing out. Seeing their stunned faces, I knew that few of these visitors had been aware of the actual consequences of war. They looked at us, and we looked briefly at them. Neither group seemed to have the impulse to speak to the other. I had the sense that I was witnessing a scene that had played out many times in prior wars: politicians belatedly confronting the real consequences of their decisions to escalate to war.

The dignitaries were certainly not asked to go along with me to Graves Registration detail (i.e. the morgue), which could be one of my assignments on any particular day. The Graves tent, located adjacent to the supply office, was across a bridge and separated from the C Med hospital. It contained the bodies of Marines who had recently died in the field, zipped into green body bags and waiting to have their personal identifications reviewed and their bodies readied to fly home to the United States. This job, considered the hardest duty of all, was to unzip each of the body bags and to fill out the official death report for each dead Marine. Graves was not a welcoming area, but it did have the distinction, along with the OR and ICU, of having the only other air-conditioning unit on the base. The tent was partly out of sight on the down slope of a berm, a descent that required the person entering the tent on foot to step down into the working area, which was where the bags were lined up on the floor.

After one of these dignitary tours, the faces of the politicians were still in my thoughts when I opened that day's first body bag. The odor of death rose from it…pungent, appalling. Although I had experienced it before, I almost fell back onto the ground. This young man had died from a gunshot wound that had entered his forehead and exited the back of his neck. All I could do was silently ask myself: *Could he possibly have anticipated this outcome when he signed up?* His hopes of becoming a farmer, a teacher or pharmacist, and perhaps of having a great love in his life, were gone. Now all that remained of him was his badly damaged corporeal leavings, the body bag, and the recollections of him that would reside in the memories of those he had left behind, both in Vietnam and the United States.

Few of us are prepared for the contemplation of the unfathomable space between the living person and the dead body. Even now, after a lifetime of being exposed to that transformation, it still stuns me. In those moment, one simple truth is always inescapable for me: the life force— perhaps that is what people mean by a "soul"—leaves the body at death, once and for all, and returns to the mystery of the universe.

Each time I saw one of those body bags, it was a reminder to me that I had to make my life add up to something. It was just as I had felt when my medical school roommate, Steve Yeoman, had died while remaining so determined, even frantic to become a doctor. I wanted my life to be an act of gratitude for the very gift of life. The question was always "What can I do?" And the answer was daily in front of me at C Med: To alleviate the suffering that surrounded us.

CHAPTER XI

Naval Hospital Site Under Attack

Multi-Pronged Attack on Greater Da Nang Base

Under cover of 60mm mortar fire, a VC raiding party of 90 men struck the Marble Mountain Air Facility, destroying one third of the helicopters and badly damaging the partially constructed Naval hospital. U.S. losses were 17 dead and 91 wounded.

—Associated Press (AP) October 28, 1965

The naval hospital was just a month from completion when it was attacked.

The construction site had been deemed safe enough in the daytime because of the large numbers of Seabee construction teams working. But when they returned up the road to their more secure base camp each evening, the hospital sat alone, vulnerable to attack. It was located at the extreme southern margin of the patchwork of tents and Quonset huts that were the Da Nang base. To the south was a free-fire zone. To the west, over a 200-foot high ridge, was the slow-moving water of the Han River estuary, and a small village. The Marines called this "Tiger Country" because it was under Viet Cong control. The only safe side of the hospital was across the road to the east and north, where Marine bunkers surrounded the helicopter base. In checking on the security, the Navy was told by the 3rd Marine Division command that, due to a lack of personnel, perimeter protection at the hospital site during construction was up to their commander—the same doctor who had dropped everything to kindly drive me to C Med when I first arrived in Da Nang—Canaga. He ran a medical team of twenty corpsmen. Being an internal medicine specialist first and a hospital administrator second, Canaga had been given minimal advice about or training on what to do if the hospital were attacked. The corpsmen's training had been primarily as medics, not as guards. At night, the corpsmen sat in the bunkers they had dug around the perimeter. These were holes in the ground covered with stout logs, with sand bags placed on top of the logs. The holes were connected by voice-activated phones to Canaga in the command bunker.

At C Med, our causality alarm bell rang at 2200 hours, and we all ran to triage, where Commander Wilson informed us of the urgent call for medical aid from the Seabee unit at the naval hospital. Since the helicopters were temporarily grounded, we sent our ambulances down the five-mile road to their unit. This attack on the hospital was one of the largest ever on the greater Da Nang base (and would not be equaled until 1968, during the Tet offensive).

The main targets were the two air bases: the helicopter base on China Beach and the main jet base at Da Nang, which had been launching bombing runs as far north as Hanoi. The attack on the jet base was successfully repulsed with no U.S. casualties. But, across the river, the three adjoining units—the Naval hospital construction site, the MAG 16 helicopter base, and the Seabee construction battalion base—sustained great damage. The attack began with mortars fired on each of the units, followed by about ninety Viet Cong soldiers approaching on foot, carrying satchels with explosive charges. They easily passed through the poorly guarded Naval hospital perimeter, throwing explosives into each of the buildings, and then crossed the road, where they destroyed a number of helicopters sitting on the runway. They proceeded through the adjacent Seabee compound and hit the living quarters, injuring and killing some Seabees in their bunks. The perimeter guard responded with gunfire, and the few Viet Cong survivors fled across the road and back to the river. The attack lasted sixty minutes.

Wilson ordered me to travel with the ambulances, and sent me back to my tent for my flak jacket, helmet, and side arm. I was to determine the priority for evacuation. One of the older corpsmen said he was going with me, which was reassuring. We packed extra battle dressings and IV fluids and headed to the hospital site as fast as we could. I didn't have time to be frightened, but I nevertheless recognized the possibility of a land mine on the roadway, as well as the risk of another attack. As we drove by the main air base, we heard the usual reverberating sound of howitzers firing, but there was nothing usual about that night. Luckily, there was no traffic, and no one ambushed us. We arrived at the gate of the Seabee compound, now lit only by the headlights of the ambulances, and could barely see the shadowy movements of men walking between the tents. The Seabee guards at the gate directed us to their helicopter pad, where we found sixty wounded men already bandaged and waiting. Their voices were hushed in the darkness.

We were first shown around by flashlights. But fortunately, power was safely returned within minutes of our arrival. Based on their experience, the Marine Command knew that this attack was a suicide hit-and-run mission. They found no evidence we would be hit again that night.

There were four men with serious abdominal and chest injuries. They had intravenous fluids running, but needed urgent surgical care. The MAG 16 helicopter base had reopened by then, and we called for an air evacuation for these cases. We then loaded the walking wounded into the four ambulances, for the first of four trips back to C Med. Over the next twelve hours at C Med, we treated the sixty wounded men. I assisted in surgery from 4:00 a.m. until noon, when the final operation was completed. Our entire unit fell quiet as exhausted corpsmen and doctors simply passed out—basically right where they were in the active medical areas—many of them asleep on gurneys.

Dr. Gerald Moss arrived in Da Nang just after the October attack on the compound. He had spent the year before arriving in Vietnam at Chelsea Naval hospital in Massachusetts, learning the nuances of the new frozen blood technology. He then had been assigned to live onsite at the naval hospital in Da Nang to set up and oversee the expensive, one-of-a-kind, frozen blood-processing equipment that arrived at the same time. Moss spent each day putting the blood bank together, catching the occasional nap, and remaining for the most part awake each night in the command bunker in anticipation of another attack. The corpsmen did the same.

At a medical meeting in San Francisco in 2002, we were reunited and he told me a story. One night a few weeks after the attack, during one of Moss's routine hourly checks with the perimeter, one of the bunkers did not respond with radio contact. Moss was worried. After a number of unsuccessful calls, and fearing the worst, he broke protocol and stood up in the bunker, thus exposing himself to possible enemy fire. He yelled out, "Brudzinsky, answer the goddamn phone!" No longer asleep, Brudzinsky jumped up, said, "Sorry, sir," and then disappeared back into his hole.

After weeks of fearing imminent death, nightly, in the dark of the bunker, Moss had undergone some kind of internal change. "I didn't recognize it at the time, but that experience made life as head of a surgery department, or later still as dean of a medical school, a lot more enjoyable. I may have been the target of verbal bullets in the academy, but no one was firing an AK-47 at me."

In hindsight, I have a better understanding of how military bureaucracy works in wartime, and I am now less surprised that the defense of the hospital site was left to doctors. After I had returned from Vietnam, I learned that my father's unit had been part of the invasion of Kiska Island, one of the Aleutian chain of islands off Alaska, during World War II. Kiska had been captured by Japanese Marines in 1942, after fierce fighting on another Aleutian island named Attu, in which many American and Canadian troops had been killed. In August 1943, ninety-five ships and 34,426 troops were assembled for the attack on the Japanese soldiers stationed on Kiska. For unknown reasons, a medical battalion was sent ashore before the first wave of combat troops. Fortunately, they found that the Japanese had abandoned the island. Despite the absence of any enemy fighting, there were still close to two hundred casualties from mines, booby traps, and friendly fire. Later, I learned that, when my father was in Europe, medical personnel of the 28th Field Hospital had been sent across the Rhine before combat support troops and their protection.

CHAPTER XII

C Med, Da Nang, November 1965

A fter the attack on the Naval hospital, life returned to a
yet another onslaught of massive war wounds.

One day, a Marine arrived at C Med with most of
his legs blown off by a land mine, pressure tourniquets having
been applied to each thigh, to stop the bleeding. He was breathing rapidly. He stopped speaking, and then stopped looking
around. He had gone into shock and had lost so much blood
that his brain function was shutting down. The corpsman was
already working to get an IV inserted into his right arm, while
I assessed the shrapnel wounds in his belly, chest and left arm.
A portable bedside X-ray would have been helpful, but was not
available in triage, and we would have been foolish to move
this unstable patient, in such fragile condition, the distance to
the X-ray tent. He might need CPR at any moment. The decision of whether or not to insert a chest tube was made after we
had employed the old-fashioned technique of checking that his
trachea was in the mid-line position, and listening for equal
breath sounds in both lungs, which, if present, would tell us
that he did not need the chest tube.

His belly was not rigid, in spite of the location of the wounds,
so that the risk of abdominal organ injury moved lower on my
list of worries.

I estimated that he had lost three quarters of his blood

volume. Cardiac arrest was imminent. I needed to get a big IV line into him quickly, and to transfuse blood, or he would surely die in moments. The corpsman had not been able to find a viable site for the IV in his arm. I knew that we needed to use a larger vessel, and therefore examined his groin, and prepared it with iodine disinfectant. I couldn't feel the soft, finger-sized vein, but located it by its known proximity to the artery. I then placed the line blindly in the vein, a procedure made all the more difficult because the vein had collapsed due to severe blood loss.

After the successful insertion, he received two liters of IV salt solution, followed by type-specific blood. After five minutes and three liters of fluid infusion, his brain recovered enough from the poor blood flow for him to speak to us. What he said was mumbled, but it was a positive sign. "Good going, Marine," I said to him. "Back to the States soon."

The OR was now available, so that I could hand the patient off to the anesthesiologist, to continue to bring his fluid replacement to a safe level before surgery. On the way to the OR, the patient was X-rayed, revealing shrapnel in the abdominal cavity. In addition to amputating both his legs, we would have to explore his abdomen, and then debride his arm of dirt and shrapnel. The surgeon that day was Dr. Greg Cross, a newly arrived career Navy surgeon, who was forty years old. He and I would be working simultaneously on this man.

I was to learn in surgery that day, and in the months afterwards, that Cross was a man who never lost his composure. In addition, he was more neatly put together than anyone in the unit. The rest of us would regularly be dressed in cut-offs and Ho Chi Minhs, while Cross always wore proper Navy clothing. Vietnam is a very hot country, literally. We used to kid him that the sweat marks on his shirts were smaller than anyone else's. Cross was very skilled at keeping a team working well together. He eventually took over as commanding officer at C

Med when Richard Escajeda completed his tour of duty.

To be fair, composure was the usual among all the surgeons with whom I worked in Vietnam. I cannot recall a single instance in which anger or blame was visited by a surgeon on any of the other physicians or corpsmen with whom we worked. Everyone took responsibility for his own actions. The immediacy of the war, and our need for constant focus on the very real issues at hand, brought out the best in the entire team.

With this particular patient, Cross started exploring the belly, while I debrided the left leg. The first step in the debridement was to recognize and remove any dead tissue, which in such cases is bloodless, limp and ground-up. It reminded me, literally, of road-kill. I was trying to make sense of the cross-sectional anatomy of his leg, which had been radically re-arranged by the savagery of his wounds. Normally, each muscle is surrounded by fascia, bundled with adjacent nerves, arteries, and veins. But nothing was normal with this exploded knee joint. What was left of the man's leg was shredded, and I needed to find some normal anatomy in order to get oriented. Strands of fascia began to look like nerves. Everything was mixed together.

I started talking aloud to myself. "Is this the popliteal artery?" I came across a glistening flat structure. "Is this a misplaced joint capsule, or the interior of a vein?"

Waldron, giving anesthesia to the patient, and never shy, peered over the screen with a cigarette in his mouth. "Ward-o, get your ass in gear."

He could say this and I would take it as a brother would, to get me back into action. But I remained confused. Cross looked over at me, sensing that I had stopped making progress. He pointed out the obvious: A stump at a joint would never be suitable for prosthesis because it was so bulbous, and offered no muscle or skin for coverage.

We knew we were near the time limit for the leg tissue

below the tourniquet to remain viable. I began to visualize what I wanted the stump to look like, and realized that I needed to cut the femur bone where it narrowed above the joint. I needed to become the sculptor of a stump that, when healed, would best fit a prosthesis. I let the tourniquet pressure ease, then found the cluster of artery, vein, and nerve behind the knee joint, traced the artery to where it had a pulse, and sutured it with nylon. These sutures would remain easily visible, so that the surgeon doing the next stage of the process could find them. I managed the nerve and vein in a similar fashion, and pushed all three out of the way, so that the bone could be cut with a saw without injury to any of the remaining tissue. To finish the resection, I used a wire-saw with teeth that would cut in both directions when pulled back and forth, like dental floss. The surgery to close the muscle and skin would come at the next stage, five days later, if the wound remained free of infection and dead tissue.

By the time I finished the left leg, Cross was done with the abdomen, where he had found and repaired the patient's injured small bowel. Due to his experience, Cross was a much faster operator than I was. So I assisted him on the right leg. I found myself very attentive to the little steps that Cross made, and the efficiencies of them, which I had not been aware of moments before when I had been plodding through the patient's left leg on my own. This reverse sequence of training—do one, then see one done—placed me in a heightened learning mode. I watched how Cross placed the needle in the tip of the needle holder, and then advanced the needle to a position in the tissue that permitted him to grasp it cleanly in one move, eliminating the many extra moves that I would have made. I noted his delicate, respectful handling of the tissue.

When we finally emerged from the OR, in late afternoon, two and a half hours had simply disappeared. This scene would become increasingly frequent.

I wrote to Nancy one day in late October: "If I were a poet, I would write you a poem depicting the Marines' life in the jungle… Sitting out on the four-holer with diarrhea, soaking wet in the constant rain, trying to get over a cold that has you exhausted, and knowing the bed you have to go back to is cold and wet… I would try to describe the unease in all the men, and Hanoi Hanna broadcasting that C Med better get ready for work tonight. Today, I'm reading *Yankee from Olympus* (by Catherine Drinker Bowen) about Oliver Wendell Holmes, where it mentions being wounded and 16,000 men being lost in a month in the Civil War. I know a little more now what that cold number means."

A few days later, as I was waiting at triage for a helicopter to unload the next wounded man, four men bearing a stretcher came running up, stopped short of the treatment area, placed their patient on the ground and signaled urgently to me. One of the bearers was a Marine captain, who said tersely, "Give him morphine, just morphine."

I pulled back the blanket and saw wounds that still flash in my nightmares.

From his navel down, the Marine was an unrecognizable bloody pulp. Although he was alive, he was unsalvageable. Also, he was not the usual kind of wounded young Marine that we saw. His hair was gray, and so was his face. He uttered no sound.

I learned from the captain that this patient was his commanding officer, a bird colonel (which is to say a full colonel, one step below the rank of general). He had been the first man off the helicopter in a new landing zone, there to lead a large assault. But the place had proved to be a trap. He had bolted through chest high grass and tripped a mine…in full view of his whole company.

In what I knew was a profound show of respect, the captain

had accompanied him to the hospital.

The captain was badly shaken, but in control of himself and of the situation. This was just the second colonel that I had ever treated, and the first one to be wounded on the ground while actually leading an attack. I myself nearly vomited when I first saw the wounds. I had to turn and walk away a moment, simply to regain my composure.

It was clear that the colonel was mortally wounded, and in this moment, I desperately wished that he could die in a more civilized setting, with his family around him for comfort. That this man with such terrifying wounds was close to my own father's age even further stunned me.

We gave the colonel morphine. He died quietly. There was little else we could do.

Forty years were to pass before I was able to describe to Nancy the hopelessness of this scene. It was a horror that had awakened me many, many nights. The image of that officer's wounds and of the life draining from him has never left me.

At home, in private practice after the war, I would sometimes have the job of sitting with the family of a deceased patient, as they absorbed the news that their loved one had not survived some particular illness or accident. As hard as that terrible moment is, telling the family of the situation personally, and verbalizing the loss, creates a moment of closure for them. It does the same for the doctor.

Closure simply did not happen in Vietnam.

In Vietnam, there was no family waiting with whom I could share the loss. We could barely even imagine the families at home. Only later, in a quiet moment in my tent looking past the perimeter bunker and over the water-soaked rice paddies, would I think of my Dad and, in those moments, I came to understand what he had endured in war. I now saw why he had chosen to spare us from what he had experienced. At times, it may have felt to him as it sometimes felt to me now, as if he were two different people: the man who left for the war, and the man who came back. He knew that we had expected the same father to return. So he did what many of the men of the World War II generation did upon their arrival home: he pretended to be the man that we had known, and he hoped that we would never have to see what he had seen.

CHAPTER XIII

Dad's Experience of War

My father was physically absent from my childhood from 1942 to 1945, when I was between the ages of four and seven. As I look back at his silence about war, I realize that his lack of communication about his experiences in France and Germany during World War II was not only to protect us, but was also due to his having blocked the processing of it himself. I now know that, although he was so attuned to the suffering of others, he was not attuned to his own.

I remember the palpable sadness that on occasion emanated from his deep brown eyes. Sometimes he would be staring out the window or at the opposite wall, and we could see that he was experiencing something that he could not share. As children, we wanted to crack the protective shell that Dad had placed around himself, to give him some needed joy and love. My mother would often give him long full-body embraces upon his evening return from work, to the hoots, I admit, of my sisters and me. But we understood that there was a need for such affection. Oftentimes after dinner, my sisters and I would comb his hair and rub his back and feet.

My math teacher for seventh and eighth grade, who was also my high school basketball coach, had been a Marine during World War II, and had fought in the battles of Guadalcanal and Iwo Jima. On some days, he would get distracted from the math lesson, and tell battle stories to the entire class. I would beg Dad for similar stories, but he would only talk about the living conditions and the efforts to stay warm in the winter in Kiska and France, or the pranks the men had played on each other.

The one detailed story of the Normandy casualties that Dad did tell was of the sudden appearance, late in the battle, of a soldier wounded by a wooden bullet. The bullet's entry point was typical of any such wound, but there was no exit point to be found. These bullet trajectories did not show up on x-ray either...another mystery for the surgeons. Without both the entry and exit points, the attending surgeons hadn't been able to establish the likely path of the bullet, in order to make an initial, accurately placed incision into the wounded area.

The mystery had been solved when they had proceeded, and opened the wound to find shrapnel made of wood. This, of course, is invisible to x-rays. Later they heard that the Germans had run out of the lead to make metal bullets, and had resorted to actually using in battle the wood bullets more usually employed for practice rounds in training. Wood bullets were accurate only at close range, and when the skirmish was fought at such close range, they were quite deadly.

Before going to college, while looking through some old photographs, I found a news photo of Dad and six other soldiers taken in June, 1944, in southern England. They were unloading some of the first casualties from Normandy. All the doctors looked somber, their eyes focused on one wounded soldier covered by a blanket as he was carried on a stretcher from the airplane to the triage area. When I asked Dad to tell me about the scene, he took a quick look at the photo and turned away. "Those men were wounded forty-eight hours earlier, and were in terrible shape." He then got up and walked to the porch, staying outside for some minutes. I knew not to ask for more.

On October 22, 1944, when I was six years old, my father had written a letter to me from France. It was accompanied by a photo of him in uniform, wearing a Red Cross insignia on his left arm. The French countryside looked to my six year-old eyes like a rough place to fight. The letter was written on a piece of thin parchment paper, and as I look at it now, I realize it may have been handled by censors, as was all mail from the war zone to home. "I'm living in the same kind of tent I was living in when we landed on Kiska, except the floor here is dirt. When I get home, I will help you put up a tent in the back yard. Ward, I'm depending on you to help your mother."

Stoicism characterized my father's generation, and seemed especially pronounced among the veterans. Shortly after my mother's death in 1994 (she was eighty-four years old). I returned home for a visit, and went with Dad and our lawyer to the bank, to document the contents of a safety deposit box. I had always felt that my mother had been the spiritual force in the family, and worried now that my dad would be lost without her. A family trust that my parents had set up some years before needed to be reexamined, given my mother's passing. When the bank officer brought the box to us, I saw that it was filled with life insurance policies that Dad had purchased just before he had left with his hospital unit, to go ashore at Normandy in 1944. The bank officer, a woman, had known Mom and, of course, knew of her death. As she opened the box, Dad put his hand on hers and said, "Remember the night I sat with you next to your mother when she was dying?"

The woman, reminded of that scene and mindful of Dad's loss, began suddenly to sob, and then Dad himself cried openly. It was one of the few such displays of emotion I ever saw from him.

After Mom died, when my sisters and I would tell Dad, over the phone or upon ending a visit, that we loved him, he was not able to respond, and could not say that he loved us, even though it was obvious that he did. I admired my father immensely, but I knew enough about mental health to see the price he was paying for not being able to uncover the unspeakable sadness that he was carrying.

Only after my return from Vietnam could I truly understand the pain that Dad, from his experience of war, had held so closely inside. Now, when I reread my letters home from Vietnam, I can see that, although my descriptions of life there during that year had been factual, I had made only the barest mention of the actual horror I was seeing. I know that I did not personally register the emotional toll on me at the time, and it now seems obvious to me that my neglect was self-protective.

Thirty-five years after my return, I began to realize that I had become just like my dad in his stoicism and sadness, and that, like him, I harbored what was essentially a groundswell of unprocessed emotion. This heavy layer of sadness would openly express itself only periodically, like when I was watching a war movie or, rarely, glimpsing some particular moment in an episode of *MASH* on television, or hearing the Marine Corps band playing at some televised national event. At such moments, suddenly, it would become too painful for me to stay in the room.

At some point, any image of any kind that would send me back to Vietnam would physically choke me up. I knew that I had to do something about this. The realization of my unprocessed emotion eventually lead to my reading the old letters I had sent to Nancy and my family and the resulting desire to share the experience through writing.

CHAPTER XIV

Attack on Our Perimeter

One night in late-October 1965, soon after the attack on the MAG 16 Helicopter Base, a Viet Cong force of more than fifty men carried out a night attack on a company of the 1st Marine Battalion on Hill 22, within a mile of our hospital. Sixteen men died, and we treated forty-one wounded. Two days later, we received warnings from the Recon Battalion to expect the Viet Cong to invade our perimeter. There were no specific directions from C Med's commander, aside from advice that we all wear helmets and flak jackets, and sleep near our weapons.

Before Waldron and I turned in that night, we cleared out our accumulated trash, and reinforced the sand bags around the perimeter of our foxhole. With rain coming almost daily, there was standing water in the hole, which made our anticipation of spending the night in it a dismal proposition.

After an hour of hearing the sporadic "pop-pop" of single shots from beyond our perimeter, fifty yards away, we heard repeated sudden bursts of automatic fire. That sound carries an urgency that one never forgets. Since we had gone to bed with our boots on, we just grabbed our equipment, guns and ponchos, and made the bunker our home. By hunching down like a baseball catcher, sitting on my heels and leaning back against the muddy wall, I was able to stay somewhat dry. At least my butt was dry. Every five minutes, parachute flares lit up the rice paddies beyond our perimeter. Between squalls of rain, the flares reflected light from the low-lying clouds. Tracers from small-arms fire crossed the sky. When I looked toward the perimeter, I could see muzzle flashes from the Marines' rifles. The pace of the 105 howitzer firing also picked up.

There was occasional movement within the compound, which did not seem hostile, and was probably from other doctors trying to find their bunkers. I was not about to get out of the foxhole to find out for certain. Hours later, someone rushed toward us from the hospital side, and in the dark we couldn't see who it was. We all froze, but he turned out to be a corpsman looking for Waldron, who was needed in the OR. How easy it would have been for the corpsman to be shot by a nervous, inexperienced doctor.

In the long hours of uncertainly and tension that night, I tried to calm myself by imagining that I was holding Nancy next to me on her couch on 42nd Street, or of being a teenager again playing with my dogs in the back yard in Iowa. At about 4 a.m., a medevac helicopter landed, and people started moving around within the base. At breakfast later, we learned that a number of Viet Cong had been shot during the attack, and we all voiced an even greater appreciation than we had in the past for the presence of our Marine guards.

After this attack, I asked my brother-in-law to send me a multi-shot 12-gauge shotgun, which arrived a few weeks later. I spent a moment every night for the rest of the year imagining a Viet Cong firing into the tent, and I practiced how I would roll onto the floor as I grabbed the shotgun. That loaded shotgun allowed me to sleep more comfortably the rest of my tour.

Later, when my children were young and exploring the house, I got rid of it. I had no particular explanation for why I had held onto the shotgun for so many years, but I realize now that on some level I was still expecting to be attacked. Once, when my son was six years old and frightened by a bad dream, he ran into our room and shook my arm. I cried out in alarm and tackled "the intruder." In my confusion, I had been back in that trench at C Med, and my son was a Viet Cong trying to strangle me.

I am sure that I frightened him as much or more than he frightened me.

As the monsoon season continued, our clothing was constantly wet from walking to and from triage, OR, and the mess hall. We could dry our clothes out only as we were working in the tents. Creatively, we sometimes used the dryer that had been designed for developing X-rays to dry our underwear. Along with rain came the loss of reliable mail delivery, and less fresh food. Our general mood spiraled downward as a result. People ate in silence without the usual kidding.

Mail delivery occasionally became so irregular that I would get nothing for several days, and then receive three letters at once. Sometimes the mail would come out of sequence, and cause much confusion and many misunderstandings. Mail call was the peak moment of the day for us; without letters, we easily felt forgotten. Letter exchanges allowed us to transport our thoughts to safer places, away from where we were at the moment, back to places back in the States. This regular and healthy routine acted itself out in every tent throughout the base, after supper and before dark, when the action of the war would often take a pause. At that point, I wrote to Nancy daily, and to my parents weekly. If I did not have a new letter from Nancy on a particular day, I would reread an old one.

The monsoons reduced the number of supply flights that could land at the Da Nang base. The roads were mired in mud, and truck traffic slowed. When we were low on drugs, IV needles and bandages, helicopters would deliver emergency supplies, which assured us we were not cut off completely. But even when the weather was fine, C Med was chronically short of OR equipment. We would find ourselves without functioning retractors, which were used for keeping the abdomen open during surgery, bone rongeurs for opening and extending the bony exposure to the brain, and tubing for the water-seal drainage that was required for chest injuries. All these items were subject to breakage from heavy use, and many items, like the chest-tube apparatus, would go to the Philippines with the particular Marines who were being evacuated. Without that chest tube and water seal, those men would have suffered a re-collapse of the affected lung during the air evacuation to Clark Air Base.

In surgery, when we needed an instrument that wasn't there, the common response from the assisting corpsmen was, "It's on back order, doctor." Invariably, the phrase would be voiced with an exasperated, ironic—and even humorous—tone, the concept of the "back order" being a constant for us. But indeed it was part of the military ethos that we could run this operation with whatever we had, and we had developed pride in our ability to get by.

For example, when all our self-retaining retractors were worn out from constant use, those of us working in other tents would be called to the OR, to manually hold the abdominal incisions open for the surgeons. As our specialized non-crushing clamps, used for holding bowels closed, all broke, we padded standard tissue clamps with rubber tubing to prevent injury to the bowel wall. Going through the standard channels to resupply our OR could take months. So other sources were used when we could. Fortunately, Escajeda was a savvy commander, and knew how to use the back-channel delivery system. He miraculously produced a bipolar cautery unit, essential for brain surgery, soon after our neurosurgeon finally arrived. The Navy had said it would take months to procure that item. But Escajeda seemed to know the secret of working with the

Seabees, who were in charge of the port of Da Nang, and who could always come up with what was needed.

Another avenue of procurement of which we took advantage was our transfer of those patients that went to Clark Air Base in the Philippines. Many evacuations to Clark required a doctor, when the patients were in fragile shape. That lucky physician was given a supply wish list to carry with him.

The C Med physician that arrived at Clark would have been a sobering sight, dressed in a bloodstained, unwashed green field uniform, fatigue and sleep-deprivation written across his entire demeanor. Nonetheless, he would still be totally focused on his unstable patient. The staff at Clark wanted to help us in any way they could. But, because of procurement regulations, they could not officially give us supplies. Regularly, however, they would show us where the supply room was, and then walk away, leaving the door open. Given the dire condition of the wounded patients that we brought to them, they well understood our situation.

Nearly every day we cared for people on the verge of death. At times it was overwhelming, and I would close my eyes for a few seconds, hoping to make the right decisions for the Marine in front of me. I was painfully aware of my limits. No doubt my colleagues were going through a similar kind of agony, although we never talked about it. Our patients simply died or lived. None of us kept a tally.

There is a cliché in the military that there are no atheists in foxholes. I don't know about that, but I do know that most Marines, other soldiers, and their caregivers all had quite deep thoughts about their own frailty and the meaning of their lives. I had grown up in a religious family, in a church-going community, and very much wanted to keep the belief of my childhood, of an all-powerful God that would intervene in daily life. But in Vietnam, I found that I had to change one unrealistic expectation of mine: that, if I prayed enough, God would always respond with a miracle. I was very conscious that now, in those moments in which I looked away from the enormity of the injuries before me on the operating table, I could no longer say the words, "Please, God, save this man." It seemed like folly to me, to beseech the Almighty for something that was impossible. Many of these injuries were simply beyond salvaging.

In those moments of crisis, I needed and found a source of calm in a kind of meditative thought that focused me on how I could be of help and what was within my control. I turned to the prayer of St. Francis: "Make me an instrument of thy peace." This is language that any surgeon in Vietnam would well understand, and it became my silent mantra. I couldn't save every Marine. I could only do my best. That was all I had the power to do.

The evening time spent writing letters and reviewing the day was inherently introspective for me, and I came to an understanding that each of us has been given the gift of life and, with it, the choice to live a productive one. My experiences shifted my belief to be that prayer mainly benefits the person praying. I frequently witnessed wounded Marines being calmed by saying the Twenty-Third Psalm aloud with the chaplain: "Yea, though I walk through the valley of the shadow of death, I will fear no evil: For thou art with me."

I, too, was calmed in those moments, reminding myself again that I was just an instrument. In Vietnam I held myself together with two important understandings: that I wished to be a good surgeon, and that I wanted to embody the personal sacrifice that is central to the practice of medicine. I did not understand why the young men under my care had to suffer, but I did—faithfully—try to care for those who needed help.

Long after the war, whether in private practice, engaged in university teaching, or operating on strangers or friends, I continued to follow the spiritual path that I had discovered in Vietnam, and that I remained determined to follow. I've heard many last-minute pleas from a husband, wife, or parent, just as I am embarking on a very risky operation on their loved one: "Doctor, this person is my whole life." And I always answer, "You know I will do my best." It has always been the truth, and I have realized that is all I can ask of myself.

CHAPTER XV

The Chaplains

"There will never be an end to my tour in Vietnam—one can't end that to which one has given so much of himself."
                    —Fredrick Whitaker, Navy chaplain.
From *Chaplains with Marines in Vietnam* by Commander Herbert L. Bergsma, Chaplain, U.S. Navy. Published by U.S. Marine Corps, 1985.

In my first days in the triage unit at C Med, I was surprised by and doubtful of the value of the chaplain at the bedside. They played a role with which I had not been familiar in civilian emergency rooms. I noticed that, in Vietnam, none of the more experienced doctors were bothered by the chaplains' speaking to the wounded men, despite the chaplains' lack of medical training. However, I quickly came to see the value of their presence, especially as they engaged in quiet, calming conversation with the wounded, as well as helping with ancillary tasks like the removal of weapons and clothing.

I am surprised by my inability to speak about an individual chaplain by name. This inability has more to do with the character and the demands of trauma resuscitation than with any lack of admiration for the role that the chaplain played in those life-and-death times. In the acute trauma care setting, in both warfare and civilian settings, friendship and interpersonal relations among the shifting cast of characters is limited by what is required for the saving of lives.

In our situation in Vietnam, each person at the bedside had a job to do, and was respected and trusted for what he added to the team. In an odd way, the development of a deeper connection with each other was frozen in place by the formality of the tasks that worked so well in the triage unit. This does not mean that we did not develop favorites, or that we did not give friendly greetings to those same team members in the mess hall or on the volleyball court. I was called "doc" or "doctor," the chaplains were called "chaplain," and the corpsmen by a first or last name. Any talk about our former life or loved ones at home, or probing for any other personal information, was strictly limited. We were working as an efficient unit for hours at a time, but rarely spoke to each other by name. It was as if we were actors on a stage, doing the same play night after night. When the event was over, we went back to our own private lives, and shut ourselves down emotionally under the weight of the scene we had witnessed.

Knowing as we did that the wounded had sacrificed so much for us, we held enormous respect for them. They had done their job, and now we would do ours. The chaplains often would be outside triage, standing by the wounded as they waited on their stretchers in line for surgery. They comforted them, something that we were unable to do because of time and the urgency of the moment. The chaplains usually called the marines "son." That word "son"—such a comforting word—humanized the setting and made it feel as though all of us, together, were truly a kind of family.

One of the scenes that became pivotal to my appreciation of the work of chaplains occurred just weeks into my time at C Med. It was a moonless night. Among other causalities, we were in the process of triage with a man with a head wound that had caused significant brain loss. He was still breathing, but not moving or speaking. At the same time, we had a lineup of serious cases waiting to go to the OR who would not survive without surgery.

In these situations of limits to manpower, resources and time, the decision of who gets treated—and who does not—is made by the chief surgeon, which in this case was Escajeda. These kinds of decisions are constant, challenging, and painful, and must be made in warfare. For this particular brain-injured Marine, Escajeda ordered "comfort care." This meant that we would stop aggressive resuscitation efforts for him, and focus on other wounded who had better survival prospects.

We ordered morphine for the man's comfort, and the chaplain quietly moved up to the stretcher and said that, even though the Marine's dog tags listed him as Catholic, and although he, the chaplain, was a Protestant minister, he wished to give the man his last rites as his Catholic faith prescribed. The chaplain's gesture was lovely, and we all remained quiet during the blessing.

Afterwards, the chaplain turned to Escajeda and respectfully nodded his head, acknowledging his understanding of the difficult decision that Escajeda had just made.

Later, after another long siege of wounded men, whom we were still in the process of stabilizing, yet another chaplain went outside the triage entrance to where four green body bags had been deposited the previous hour. They were heavy with the remains of the dead. They had been off-loaded from helicopters, with some of the wounded that we had just treated. The chaplain stood by each one and said a prayer of gratitude for the life lived. He then opened each bag and searched each man's clothing for personal identifying information, particularly individual addresses, so that he could notify that particular Marine's family. He knew that this would also be done by Graves Registration. But, as important as the work is that Graves Registration does, it lacks a personal touch. That chaplain would write those letters voluntarily. He was not required to do so. He would do it simply as an act of kindness to the families.

That night I pondered the loving concern that that chaplain had for those dead men and their families, and how hard it would be for him to find the appropriate words for the letters he would write and send to them.

I wrote about them in a letter to Nancy, "The chaplains are amazing. I hear them praying aloud, while it is life-or-death that I get a big IV going. Of course, I fail starting some IVs, and the men die right when I am looking for another site."

CHAPTER XVI

Nancy

10/24/2019

I n November 1965 it was my turn to take a severely wounded patient on the eight-hundred-mile flight to Clark Air Force Hospital. The Marine who needed my escort had been shot in the neck. The only way to control his bleeding had been to ligate the internal carotid artery, where it was torn and hemorrhaging. We had halted the bleeding, but that had produced a stroke (a known risk in such cases) that had left him comatose and in need of ventilation via endotracheal tube. In those days, we did not have portable ventilators. So it was my job to hand-pump a breathing bag for him, continuously for the six hours to the Philippines. At the time, we did not have a neurosurgeon or neurologist for advice. But since our patient was so young, we hoped that there was a small chance of recovery. Once at Clark, I was treated by the staff there with great respect, for having gotten my patient there alive and, more generally, for working in a war zone. In turn, I expressed great appreciation for the niceties they provided me of a tablecloth, silverware, a hot meal, a hot shower, and a clean bed.

Also while there, I reached Nancy by shortwave radio and a phone patch (which meant a voice delay), and we talked about our marriage. We had written back and forth to each other about it. But to this day she teases me that, while I talked about getting married during that phone call, I did not actually ask her directly to marry me, but rather just assumed what her answer might be. In my defense, it was very awkward to speak of such big issues over shortwave, with a bunch of men standing around in line and listening in on my big moment. I did ask her what kind of ring she wanted, and I purchased one at the Post Exchange, and mailed it to her apartment in Philadelphia. She was still working as a nurse at HUP, and taking night classes at Penn. The box containing the ring was labeled and insured. Nancy told me later that, as he handed it to her, the mailman made a guess, and told her with a smile, "I think you will probably like what is in this."

I wrote this letter home to my parents:

November 10, 1965

Dear Mom and Dad,

About the ring and the decision—I think you are right, the war has hastened the decision, but in a good way. It has forced maturity on us. The compression of time plus the daily letters have clarified what is important.

I would have preferred to bring Nancy to Iowa to meet you first— the timing of the draft notice was just as I returned to Philly from my visit with you on July 4th. The rest of the time before I shipped out was a whirlwind of falling madly in love. Even though we first met last September, the looming separation has had an impact.

I am a different man than the one you last saw, and I know I want her with me the rest of the way. Nancy is one of those refreshingly good people like both my sisters, and I want you to love her as much as I do.

Love,
Ward

CHAPTER XVII

Crossing the Line, Da Nang, December 1965

I felt that my professional competence as a surgeon had come into its own during my months at C Med. I wrote to Nancy that "my on-the-spot training is making me a bold, decisive and fast surgeon." There was nonetheless another important lesson still to be learned and understood.

As the rain continued into December, I began volunteering at the Vietnamese civilian hospital, the United States Overseas Mission (USOM) in downtown Da Nang. I was afforded this respite from clinic and triage time because of the arrival of four new doctors at C Med, and partly because of the more enlightened military command strategy, of using the skill of the doctors and dentists as a gesture of goodwill to the people of Vietnam. The civilian hospital was under-staffed, but frequently supplemented by U.S. civilian volunteer surgeons. We were encouraged by Escajeda to help out with the backlog of work there, when it was quiet at C Med.

The gray, cement-block building was old, run down, and crowded. The beds were so tightly spaced that it was hard to get between them to examine a patient. We became accustomed to the sounds of the Vietnamese language as the interpreters helped with their stories. The dominant smell was of dirty clothing and linen, mixed with that of the cook-fires used for the food the families camped in the courtyard were preparing.

One entire ward was filled with two patients per bed, each patient facing the opposite direction from each other. Some beds had three patients in them. From above each bed hung a jumble of traction ropes and pulleys, to be used for stabilizing fractured femurs and other bone injuries. All nursing care, bathing, and feeding were left to the families.

One of the notable cases that I had was the repair of the radial nerve on a young boy who had suffered a deeply lacerated arm in an accident three weeks earlier. The radial nerve is one of three major nerves that control function of the hand and arm. The boy could no longer extend his wrist as a result of the injury. I had seen such a procedure performed at HUP before I had left, but I had never performed one myself. It is one thing to witness a procedure, and another thing to decide to go ahead with it without the experience of actually having been trained in doing it. I had examined the boy several days earlier, and discussed the procedure with one of the C Med surgeons. It was a matter of exploring the injured area, identifying the severed radial nerve and reconnecting it.

Nerve repairs on Marines were performed up to a month post-injury, after they had been evacuated back to the States, and then done by a hand or plastic surgeon specialist who had access to resources not available to us in the field, such as an operating microscope and postoperative physiotherapy.

I did the repair on the boy's arm, found the ends of the cut nerve, and sewed them together. It appeared to work. Nerves grow slowly (one millimeter a day), so it would take months to determine how successful the repair was in returning function to the hand. Perhaps because of my technical success with that radial nerve repair, I was asked to return to the civilian hospital to explore a brachial plexus shrapnel injury, which had occurred a month before. The injury had left the man's right arm useless.

The brachial plexus looks like a complex wiring box. The nerves exit from the bony spine that lies at the junction of the neck and the chest, in the space above the clavicle. They then wrap around the artery and vein, and follow these vessels down the arm. Gaining surgical access is difficult, requiring a very small incision to an area that is a complex entanglement of nerves and blood vessels. I liken this procedure to that of building a ship in a bottle.

By accepting the challenge, I seriously overestimated my skill, and underestimated my lack of experience. The flattery of being asked had indeed clouded my judgment. What had resembled an electrical box before the gunshot wound, now, after a month of healing, looked as though cement had been poured into the box, fusing all the structures together. The first nerve we found was too close to the spinal cord to graft.

The moment of truth occurred when the USOM doctor and I each found out, over the anesthetized patient, how little experience the other one had. I was in over my head. I felt like a Marine deep in a jungle having led my squad into the wrong valley. We both realized that we should not proceed, and backed out without doing any harm to the nearby major vessels.

That close call was to pay off for the rest of my career, by making me a safer surgeon. That day, I had crossed a forbidden line in surgery, where the exhilaration of my own sense of challenge betrayed my duty "to first do no harm." The maturity and wisdom of knowing when not to intervene takes time to cultivate, and surely is as valuable as the knowledge of how and when to intervene.

On Christmas Day, the temperature reached ninety degrees in Da Nang, with intermittent rain. The day came and went like every day that week, without much notice. Mom had sent me cookies, and I had forgotten to thank her. All of us in C Med were so buried in our personal loneliness and depression that we had little holiday spirit. A lightly decorated, dehydrated pine tree had been set up in the triage tent, and the cooks made the big effort, much valued by us, of serving us a lunch of turkey with cranberry sauce.

It may have been a very plain meal, but I remember it as delicious.

Many of us went outside afterwards for a game of volleyball, which remained for us at C Med the only carefree respite. The married men with children at home were the hardest hit by the fact that it was Christmas Day. All of us had been in the medical profession long enough to get used to working on major holidays, when we'd rather be at home. But the constant visual confrontation with maimed American soldiers and Vietnamese citizens had become a torment. Our time in Vietnam was stretching into a year-long sentence of macabre and joyless work.

Caring for sick children at the USOM Hospital on light days that winter did prove to be a helpful change of pace. When two teenaged siblings, suffering from massive goiters, were brought to me, I recalled my earlier humbling experience of working on the man with the injured brachial plexus, and I recognized that these children needed expert anesthesia and experienced surgeons who could do the needed procedure correctly. I arranged to bring the children from USOM to our Naval hospital, and, with the help of our trained surgeons there, removed the thyroids.

For children with burn scars, I asked for advice, and read up on plastic surgery reconstruction. Often a burned hand would have been wrapped in a bandage and, as the hand had healed, the fingers then would have sealed together like a mitt. I was able to restore functional fingers successfully to some children by using a "Z"-plasty technique (converting the longitudinal scar that crosses a joint to a zigzag).

This treatment of Vietnamese civilians made me start thinking of what kind of work I would do in the future, after the war. I wished to nurture a sense of the future because the present was already so painful.

CHAPTER XVIII

Transfer to the Naval Hospital Da Nang, January 1966

I was transferred from C Med to the now finally completed Naval hospital. Both facilities were definitely needed as the troop numbers and casualties continued growing.

As I picked up my footlocker to leave C Med, I looked out from my tent on the edge of the encampment, and past the perimeter bunker, where miles of small rice paddies receded into the distance. At the far edge of the rice paddies, the green hills and mountains of Laos, shaped like the conical hats that the Vietnamese schoolgirls wore, rose up tier beyond tier into the western sky. It was impossible not to be impressed by the resilient beauty of Vietnam, despite the ruinous conflict taking place there.

Driving east, we passed the city of Da Nang and the main air base, crossing the Da Nang River Bridge and driving onto the sandy spit of land that lay between the estuary and the South China Sea. We headed south past the camp of the Sea-bees, who were stationed on the coast, arriving finally at the Naval hospital. It was located across the road from the Marble Mountain helicopter base, where I had spent my first night in Da Nang. South of us rose the eight-hundred-foot-high volcanic rock called Marble Mountain. Full of caves, it was found after the war to have served as a Viet Cong hospital. North of us, past the turnoff to the bridge, was Monkey Mountain, which housed an American missile site and, later, an Army hospital. From the top of Monkey Mountain, one could see the busy Da Nang harbor. Of special interest to us was the Navy hospital ship, USS *Repose*, which would begin service in the harbor in March.

The three of us who had been stationed at C Med— neurosurgeon Dr. Paul Pitlyk, Waldron, and myself—joined Canaga, Moss, Adams, plus seven recently arrived doctors, to staff the Naval hospital. With our move, I felt that I had crawled out of a blood-soaked mud hole into a world with light, and clear horizons.

The new hospital was full of luxuries: hot running water, a laundry service, and a dining hall with tablecloths and fresh food. We moved into a Quonset hut that was serviced by a housecleaning team of Vietnamese women, who smiled and laughed and showed their black teeth (stained from chewing betel nut) when we thanked them. The hospital buildings were built on concrete slabs with corrugated steel roofs and small windows. There were covered walkways between each of the buildings.

As had the tent facility at C Med, the hospital faced a huge helicopter landing pad. The helicopter wind blast had been a problem at C Med, requiring a 30-foot wall between the pad and the triage tent, to keep the tents from blowing over. This blade wind was not a problem with the new Quonset huts, so the hospital pad was very close to the triage door. Triage itself was a large open room with 20 stations, each supplied for IV insertion, tourniquet application, endotracheal intubation, and chest tube insertion.

Here I worked in triage, the OR, and ICU for at least twelve hours a day, every day for the remainder of my year, as the flow of casualties into and out of our facility continued. Our procedure in triage was similar to that in C Med. The doctor who started resuscitation on a patient ran the team for that person, and asked for help when needed. If a patient had multiple wounds, we would often have three doctors and a corpsman attending to him, each working on a different extremity, or assisting. The chief surgeon oversaw the entire station during times of mass casualties, ensuring the coordination of the cases. All patients directed to surgery were taken on a gurney twenty paces up the walkway to X-ray, and then twenty paces further to the OR building, which had four rooms. Postoperative recovery and ICU was a joint unit in another building, always full with patients. Those with conditions that did not require surgery were in yet another building.

The officer's quarters, with a club and volleyball pit, were a good distance from the triage area, so that, when off duty, we now had some sense of separation from work. It felt more like working in a stateside hospital.

I worked on a long string of cases assisting Moss, with Waldron running the anesthesia. Moss was a terrific surgeon, but a humble man, with a knack for telling self-deprecating stories. For example, he told one about how, as an inexperienced medical student, he had unknowingly contaminated the surgical field during a particular operation, and had been kicked out of the OR by the surgeon, the famous Dr. Robert Zollinger, who was chief of surgery at Ohio State University Medical School.

One of the first cases we had together was a patient with multiple shrapnel wounds of the chest and belly. The Marine's abdomen was rigid, which was strong evidence that the shrapnel had injured an internal organ. It was 1966, before the advent of CT or ultrasound scans, and we needed to rely on our physical exam and X-rays (which would be taken in two views, to estimate which organs had been hit).

Early in the case, as Moss and I were exploring the patient's abdomen, Waldron said he thought the patient was developing cardiac tamponade—that is, the shrapnel had also hit the heart, and the heart was bleeding into the rigid pericardial sac.

With each contraction and leak, the heart was becoming more compressed by the blood that was filling the compartment. From his view at the head of the operating table, Waldron would have noted both the patient's dilated neck veins and his low blood pressure...signs either of a tension pneumothorax or cardiac tamponade. In this case, he could hear good breathing sounds, so he concluded that it had to be the cardiac injury.

Tamponade would be fatal if not corrected by opening the pericardium to release the pressure. Moss had been so focused on the patient's gastric injury that he was oblivious to any outside chatter. Waldron's finding, expressed in his Texas drawl, went by unnoticed. So at that point, he reached over the screen, pushed a bottle of local anesthesia in Moss's face, and said, "Since I am being ignored, you can finish the case by yourself and administer your own anesthesia."

That got Moss's attention quickly, and when we extended the incision, we found that Waldron had been correct about the tamponade. Moss was very grateful to him, and told the story of their exchange later in the officer's club. The case was a great example of the experience differential between Moss and Waldron at that time. Waldron had been in Vietnam for four months doing anesthesia for many surgeries each day, whereas Moss had been tied up getting the new hospital set up, and had not been working in the operating room. Waldron was by now so aware of a patient's true condition moment to moment that he was operating on instincts, a skill Moss himself would soon acquire.

CHAPTER XIX

Neurosurgery in Da Nang

Paul Pitlyk was the first and only neurosurgeon in I Corps during my tour in 1965 and '66. He was a big-hearted and friendly man. He had not been drafted, rather he had volunteered for the Navy. In those years, communication between Washington and Vietnam, as well as between the Navy and the Marine Corp, was erratic, being adversely affected by the very rapid build-up of American forces. Pitlyk's orders to Vietnam had been like mine and Waldron's. We were to report to the Naval hospital in Da Nang. But when Pitlyk had landed in Da Nang, he had been told that the hospital had been destroyed. So, he could be taken to C Med the next day, if he so wished.

Pitlyk arrived at C Med completely unannounced. Cross, who by then had replaced Escajada as the commanding officer at C Med, was stunned by the fact that someone purporting to be a neurosurgeon had arrived. He had been making repeated requests for a neurosurgeon, and been informed by Washington after his most recent communication that it would take six months to provide one. Upon first meeting him, Cross worried that Pitlyk was an imposter, since there had been no official announcement of his arrival. When he asked Pitlyk how much training he'd had, Pitlyk, thinking he was being asked about his Camp Pendleton Marine training, and not his seven-year neurosurgery training, answered, "Two weeks." Cross jokingly responded, "Okay. Two weeks is probably adequate to learn brain surgery." Although they cleared up the misunderstanding, Cross watched Pitlyk closely during the first few cases in which he was involved, and later made much fun of himself over his initial suspicions.

Like Waldron, Pitlyk was unassuming about his rank and experience. Despite being an accomplished neurosurgeon who had undergone years of difficult specialty training, he knew the personal name of every corpsman, and addressed each one by that name.

Fresh out of residency, and without any experience with traumatic brain injuries, I had been amazed at how calm Pitlyk was when operating without the use of a bipolar cautery, which is the mainstay for controlling bleeding vessels in the brain. Blood vessels in the brain are small and fragile, and without the surrounding support tissue found in the rest of the body, do not lend themselves to being clamped or sutured for the control of bleeding. The bipolar cautery allows a surgeon to cut through brain tissue while simultaneously cauterizing the blood vessels as the dissection proceeds.

Just prior to his leaving Vietnam, Escajeda had managed to obtain a bipolar cautery through a contact he had with the Seabees. But until we got it, we had to resort to placing saline-soaked felt pledgets on each tiny bleeding site, an outdated standard from the 1940s. With suction and time, the patient's innate coagulation ability eventually stopped the blood loss.

One of the first cases on which I assisted Pitlyk still stands out clearly to me. Our patient that day, an eighteen-year-old Marine, had sustained a hit from a mortar fragment that had entered his left temple and crossed to the right temple. Now that we had a neurosurgeon, we were determined to treat these cases. The patient had a bandage on his head, and was unconscious. But he was breathing easily. I slid the bandage off the entrance wound, and found under it an oozing mixture of blood and what looked literally like cream of mushroom soup. Pitlyk may have uttered a whisper of personal reservation that this appeared to be an already fatal injury. But his judgment—and ours—was clouded by our new expectations, given the recently arrived bi-polar cautery technology and Pitlyk's command of the situation. As we were mapping out the surgery, one of the patient's pupils became fixed and dilated. He needed surgery and decompression urgently, if he were to be saved. There was no time to consider what cerebral function he might be left with if he survived.

We drilled four burr holes around the perimeter of the entry wound and then, using a wire saw, cut the bone, allowing us to lift off the section of the skull. Once the skull was opened, heavy bleeding poured from the track that the mortar fragment had made through the brain tissue. Stopping the bleeding then became the priority, requiring that we find the origin of the blood, and secure it. The patient's blood loss was so heavy that we were taxed with having to transfuse him quickly enough to keep his heart beating. We sucked out the liquefied, damaged brain tissue, and soon were working blindly in the bloody cavity.

Still searching for the source of all the bleeding, we finally determined that it was coming from the superior sulcus, a giant vein that drains blood from the entire brain, located between the two lobes). Pitlyk said that he had never known a tear of the sulcus to be repairable, and I was stunned by what this surely meant.

Although at this point the situation was hopeless, we could not abandon the effort to save the patient's life. Ligating the entire sulcus would not only be difficult, but would cause fatal brain swelling. The only hope was, despite Pitlyk's stated concern, to patch the hole in the wall of the vein. We had just one chance, given the rate of massive blood loss. Visibility in the bloody hole became nearly impossible. Blood was literally running off the drapes onto my surgical gown and through it, onto my belly and down my legs. I could not get out of the way of the flow. Pitlyk was able to place one stitch, but in tying the knot, the hole grew larger.

The inevitable had happened. The bleeding stopped. The EKG went flat.

There was a moment of uncomfortable silence before Pitlyk thanked us all for our help, saying, "We have lost a family's precious eighteen-year-old son." We departed one by one, to try to make sense of this waste of life, and to try to erase it from memory. The fact that we had operated on that Marine to save his life, rather than treating him as a fatality from the beginning, made the outcome immeasurably worse for all of us. We had to live with the helpless realization of not being able to stop the loss of blood. We had tried and failed. I had a nagging sense that our personal failure on that day was part of a much larger failure that none of us was yet willing to see…the possible failure of the Vietnam War itself.

During his time in Vietnam, Pitlyk brought real innovation to our approach to wartime brain surgery. He eventually found that bone chips and shrapnel could be left behind in the brain, thus avoiding collateral damage from the extensive surgery required to completely remove every stray fragment. Current antibiotics would be effective enough to prevent the feared infection that could come with any foreign bodies being retained in the injured brain. This was an idea contrary to standard operating protocols from earlier war manuals. However, over time, Pitlyk's approach proved safer and more beneficial to preserving brain function.

From that time on, I was the designated neurosurgical assistant, primarily because I was willing and very interested. I developed enough skill that, when Pitlyk fractured his hand, I was able to take over the heavy work of opening the skull, while he managed, even with his injured hand, to work on the delicate brain tissue.

At about the same time, I was appointed the ward surgical officer in charge of post-operative patients. As such, I was responsible for ordering treatments and overseeing wound care, and made rounds daily with the surgeons. After rounds, I worked in the triage intake unit, and continued to assist Pitlyk in neurosurgery as needed. With just fifteen doctors assigned to the hospital, caring for around a hundred seriously ill patients at a time, we all worked long hours.

CHAPTER XX

Wartime Research

In addition to caring for the wounded, the Naval hospital carried out medical research, and this was why Moss had been selected to set up the frozen blood technology we were now to use.

We were the first base to actively use frozen blood on a large scale during combat. The prior way of getting blood to the wounded had required a laborious system of delivery, consuming so much time that the blood was almost outdated by the time it reached us. It often had to be discarded. Frozen blood gave us a large, readily accessible blood supply for those patients needing massive transfusions. The program and technology were developed as a joint venture with Massachusetts General Hospital and Chelsea Navy Hospital in Massachusetts, and required an elaborate machine to thaw and reconstitute the red cells.

Glycerin was used as the freezing and storing agent. When blood is frozen in its native state, the water normally in blood forms sharp destructive crystals that fracture the cells. Glycerin did not solidify when frozen, so that red cells were preserved intact. The blood, stored at minus-85°C, could last five years. We no longer had to throw out such a precious resource.

Our unit also began research to find the optimal combination of IV fluids and blood, to be used in treating shock.

We carried out sophisticated measurements on cardiac output, peripheral vascular resistance, and acid-based balance. This data was still in its beginning phase when I finished my tour.

Of all the organs of the body, the kidneys and lungs stand out as acutely susceptible to poor blood flow caused by trauma, leading to shock and death. In the Korean War, as in World War II, IV saline replacement had not yet been thought of as the first step in shock prevention. In Vietnam, we paid a great deal of attention to the cellular and vascular fluid that is lost, and found that early saline replacement produced a high salvage rate for those patients in profound shock, and still saved their kidneys.

While our use of large volumes of saline kept the kidneys working, prevented renal failure, and improved survival, its use also unearthed a new shock syndrome that we called "Da Nang Lung" or "wet lung." This was a type of pulmonary edema caused by fluid leak in the lung tissue.

Our first observation of this syndrome was in an older Army Special Forces officer who became short of breath twenty-four hours post-operatively. He had received gunshot wounds in the abdomen and chest, and his lungs had filled with fluid after the surgery, as though he were undergoing heart failure. Yet we determined that his heart was fine. Eventually he died of the failure of his fluid-filled lungs to deliver adequate oxygen to his bloodstream.

Since the Vietnam War, the field of medicine has determined that wet lung is caused by the release of inflammatory molecules from large wounds. These molecules injure sensitive cells in the capillaries (small vessels) of the lungs and other organs.

We nonetheless were partially successful in treating these cases once we received mechanical ventilators, several months after this first patient had died. Even then, though, the survival rate never rose above fifty percent.

Field research in wartime has led to great innovations in the care of civilian trauma victims.

In World War I, Dr. Walter Cannon, a famous Harvard Medical School physiologist working on the front lines in France with an English surgical team, began to define "wound-shock," the collapse not accounted for by blood loss alone. The wounded patient today, we know, could be given blood and saline both, to prevent shock. But blood typing was not available for most of World War I, and the concept of IV fluid resuscitation did not exist. In 1917, Dr. Oswald Robertson set up a blood bank, and administered blood intravenously for the first time in the field hospital at Bethune, France. Other fluids were given only by mouth or rectum.

Abdominal wounds in particular were considered to be *check* fatal. In his 1945 autobiography *The Way of An Investigator*, Dr. Cannon described the hopeless, pathetic cases that had been left to die in the shock ward: "Bellies torn open...By the second day, those who had not already died were septic, weakened and calling mama or papa...a desperate depressing place."

Also, during World War I, shock had been thought to have a nervous component, exacerbated by pain and fear. Years later, in 1940, Dr. Alfred Blalock proved that an injury could result in fluid loss from the vascular system into the wound, and that the restoration of vascular volume was key to shock therapy.

In World War II, there was no designated research in the war zone. Saline was not yet being used to replace low vascular volume from blood and fluid loss. Indeed, the concept of fluid shifting into the trauma wound was not fully appreciated until the early 1960s. Plasma and poorly cross-matched blood were the only resuscitation fluids used in World War II, where, at times, blood was sucked from the open wound by the operating physicians, and transfused back to the patient, with no way to prevent bacterial contamination. The delay of six to seven hours in the arrival of World War II casualties to a major surgical hospital led to long periods with poor fluid replacement, resulting in a high rate of fatal renal failure.

The human body is 60% saline by weight. One-twelfth of that volume is in the vascular space itself. All fluids in the body must be in the correct balance, both inside and outside the cells. Indeed, all of the energy of life is directed to maintaining this balance.

Bullets, missiles, or the blast of an explosion destroy such balance in the zone of injury. That is why the entire focus of wartime medicine now is aimed at helping the body recover that balance. The transfusion of two liters of saline is one of the first responses now to most war wounds. This action both replaces lost saline to the traumatized spaces of the wound cavity, and aids the circulation. Blood transfusion and coagulation factors must follow in most cases.

Only with the Vietnam conflict did we come to fully understand the importance of all these issues.

But a great deal had been learned nonetheless during World War II. The lasting lessons from that conflict came from the far-sighted leadership of Dr. Edward Delos Churchill, an Army colonel in the medical corps who served as surgical consultant to General James H. Forsee in the North African-Mediterranean theatre. As a result of Dr. Churchill's advice, Forsee required each World War II surgical team in that theatre to record duplicate records on each patient up to and even after Victory in Europe Day. He wanted all such documentation completed before the teams were allowed to return home.

Two of the surgeons in that group, Dr. Paul Kennedy and Dr. Gordon Madding, had lived in San Mateo, California, and had written the highly-referenced chapter for the *2nd Auxiliary Surgical Group 1945*, Volume 1: Page 307 titled "Forward Surgery of the Severely Injured (1942-1945)". In that chapter, they had described war injuries to the liver, based on their review of their treatment of 830 battlefield cases. They had lectured at

Stanford several times when I had been a student and resident there in surgery, prior to Vietnam. In 2002, I visited their widows, who allowed me to read the trauma logs that the two surgeons had kept so meticulously up to date during the war, even as they had operated underground on the beachhead at Anzio.

At the end of World War II, individuals influential to military medicine, including Michael DeBakey, the noted cardiac surgeon, spoke up for field research, and as a result it was finally instituted as routine in the Korean War. One of the Korean War research teams was directed by Dr. John Howard. He was in his late eighties and Professor Emeritus at University of Ohio in Toledo, when I visited him in 2001 and spoke with him about his experiences. In Korea, his team had focused on the number of deaths resultant from renal failure in the wounded. From their research, they had discovered that a key factor had been the delay in getting fluid replacement into the wounded soldiers. Further, they saw that the delay had been the result of the inability to move the wounded men to medical facilities with dispatch. In Korea, the helicopters (employed for the first time in such a conflict) could only be used in daylight, were not equipped to land in the midst of battle, and were able to hold only one or two patients.

The research done by Dr. Howard's team made clear the need for two vital technological advances: the first in fluid replacement, the second in helicopter technology. Major medical developments came about as a result. Dialysis was added as a temporary treatment of renal failure, and new non-crushing clamps were developed, allowing primary repair of vascular injuries. Helicopters also became much more mobile and much faster.

Prior to the late 1950s, most U.S. civilian ambulances were simply funeral limousines, and therefore not supplied with oxygen or trained attendants. After the Korean War, Dr. Howard and others with war experience helped develop the prototypes of modern ambulances. These physicians were also influential in stimulating the formation of the national trauma system, which designated that regional hospitals be staffed around the clock with trained trauma surgeons and support teams.

A big advance in trauma medicine since the conflicts in Iraq and Afghanistan, as well as in civilian trauma centers, is the concept called "Damage Control Surgery and Resuscitation." "Damage Control" is the idea of performing primarily limited, but essential, smaller procedures early after wounding occurs, and then ensuring that the patient is stabilized before performing the larger reparative surgeries. This makes it possible for the patient to better tolerate the anesthesia and blood loss that goes with the reparative surgery. Another essential advance lies in replacing coagulation factors that may have been lost as a result of the wounding.

These advances in trauma treatment demonstrate a great irony of war. Yes, important discoveries are made, a generation of surgeons becomes more skilled, and their skills are taken with them beyond the war zone, back to civilian hospitals. Yet the advances are made at the expense of enormous suffering and loss of life.

CHAPTER XXI

Naval Hospital Expands, February-May 1966

American troop strength in Vietnam was expanding by many thousands each month, and would peak at 550,000 by 1968. With more men in battle, we had more injured to treat, and our beds and treatment areas were often filled beyond capacity. To handle this overflow, we were sending those patients with minor injuries and illness to the hospital ship *Repose*, in Da Nang harbor, or to hospitals in Japan, Guam, and the Philippines. When these facilities were filled, they were sent even further, back to the U.S. for treatment.

The long evacuation time for minor injuries was not efficient. We responded by opening a second 60-bed unit at the Naval hospital, in February 1966, designed for those with the potential to return to duty within two weeks. Minor extremity wounds, appendectomies, serious parasitic disease, and dehydration could all be treated here. By March of that year, however, we still had only fifteen doctors at the hospital, dealing with a serious increase in the number of patients, including two or three new head injury cases daily. Although we had already been working close to ninety hours a week, there was now a constant influx of patients needing treatment and surgery, with no downtime.

Waldron was accustomed to leaving the hospital compound when it was quiet, to lend a hand at the civilian hospital in Da

Nang. With the continuing rapid escalation of the war, though, we began to understand how truly essential he was to our own efforts. Inevitably, it seemed, we would get new cases the minute he left. Despite Waldron's good work at the civilian hospital, he and the other two anesthesiologists were finally told that they must not leave the Naval hospital grounds for any reason until they were relieved at the end of the year.

This order was not a reprimand, and Waldron was not upset by it. The need for yet another anesthesiologist was obvious. Waldron worked eighteen hours a day his entire last six months in Vietnam. Although he was my roommate in the Quonset hut in which we now lived, at times we would not see or talk to each other for a week. Work was all consuming, and as the year went on, exhaustion took its toll. Waldron lost some of his sense of humor and storytelling capacity, becoming more of a stranger, much like a combat-exhausted Marine who had been on patrol too long.

One morning in April, while we were attending to casualties in triage, a group of Seabees descended on us with an eight-year-old Vietnamese orphan. When I first saw the boy, he was in the arms of a quite huge Seabee, who was acting like a panicked father, repeating over and over, "Seizure. Can't talk."

Several more Seabees were in the group, and together they overwhelmed the triage unit. I pieced together their story, of how they had found the boy living alone at the dump several months earlier, and had brought him to the Seabee unit for lunch. The boy was so reminiscent to them of their own children back home that he won their hearts, was adopted by the whole unit, and given a place to stay.

It took a while to clear the commotion and get the boy onto a gurney, so that we could start examining him. But something strange was going on with him. With every attempt we made to move his limbs or other parts of his body, his back arched with uncontrolled spasms. Yet he seemed alert throughout. His eye movement was normal, but he looked puzzled and frightened by the loss of control of his body. He could not open his mouth or talk, yet had none of the repetitive jerking motions commonly associated with seizures. His belly was rigid, but he had no gastrointestinal symptoms or pain, thus ruling out an acute condition requiring surgery.

When I found an unclean wound on his leg, though, the diagnosis became immediately clear. The boy was suffering from tetanus. Tetanus, or the presence of the toxin tetanospasmin, is one of the most lethal microbial afflictions. It blocks one type of motor nerve group, thus producing unrestrained firing, which in this boy's case caused the locked jaw and arched back that we had observed. I conferred with the internist, who suggested a spinal tap, a precautionary procedure the results of which would allow us to rule out meningitis as a possible diagnosis. When the tap proved normal, we were given the green light to embark on the treatment of his tetanus.

None of us had ever seen it before, because in the developed world everyone is immunized from tetanus in infancy, and given boosters every ten years. There are only fifty cases of tetanus diagnosed in the U.S. every year. This boy nonetheless had classic textbook symptoms. We gave him a large dose of equine antitoxin for the tetanus, penicillin for the leg wound, and an IV drip of Robaxin to control his muscle spasms and ease his breathing. We debrided his leg wound, and then placed him in a dark quiet room, to reduce stimulation. He slowly recovered after three weeks of care, and regained the happy personality that by now had made him as much of a favorite at the hospital as he had been with the Seabee unit, to which he returned.

Tetanus is a member of the bacterial family Clostridium. Three of the four most common Clostridia species cause deaths in war zones because they flourish in dirty necrotic wounds, such as the one from which this boy had been suffering. All three produce toxins that injure the body distant from the site of the actual infection. These organisms live in the soil, particularly in places like Vietnam, which, at the time at least, was a poverty stricken country with a warm climate and agricultural land cultivated with human excrement.

Past wars had produced many cases of gas gangrene (Clostridium perfrigens), which is seen in neglected or incompletely debrided wounds. The only case of gas gangrene that I saw in Vietnam was in a civilian woman brought to the Naval hospital with a neglected wound. The infection had become activated in the dead tissue in the wound, and the toxin had killed adjacent muscle and produced gas formation in the tissue. Her wound and the surrounding area felt like popping plastic wrapping paper, due to the gas in the tissue. She was in severe pain, and the wound gave off a foul but oddly sweet odor.

She died within an hour.

A month later, I saw the boy who had had tetanus. He had come back for a follow-up visit. I had written to my father about my interest in this case, and on his recommendation, I gave the boy a tetanus booster. It was my father's belief, based on his pre-immunization experiences with cases of tetanus, that survival from the infection alone wouldn't ensure immunity, and that a delayed booster shot was necessary.

The Seabee unit, which had adopted this young man, flooded us with thanks and presents.

I've speculated about what happened to that boy, and thought of him many times. Some of the Vietnamese children who learned basic English from the American servicemen wanted to get to the United States and eventually were able to. Indeed, I have had Vietnamese patients in the United States, decades later, who had such childhood experiences. They remembered the names of the service people who had helped them during the war, like it was yesterday.

CHAPTER XXII

Saving Lance Corporal Shinneman

On the day in early April 1966 that Lance Corporal Perron Shinneman came to the naval hospital in Da Nang, I was assisting Moss on a repair of a multi-organ abdominal injury case. Our patient was the last to be treated from a squad of twelve men who had been shelled the evening before, just as they had been preparing their foxholes. They had been on a mission in a narrow river plain, ten miles northwest of Da Nang, known as Elephant Valley. That valley was, for us, a heartbreaking and regular source of casualties.

We were finishing the attachment of the colon stoma to the skin of this last patient when Moss was urgently called to triage. There, he found Shinneman in a state of shock from massive blood loss. He had stepped on a landmine, which had amputated his left leg at the thigh. The injury was so high that there was no stump around which to place a tourniquet. The bleeding was being controlled by a corpsman, who was putting pressure manually on a spurting vessel deep in the thigh. We had an empty OR and, fortunately, an anesthesiologist who could take the case. I finished the belly closure on the case we had been doing, and went straight in to see how I could help Moss.

Shinneman was being prepared for surgery. Two large IVs had been inserted, which brought his blood pressure up to 90 (a low but safe level). I took over for the corpsman who was still compressing the bleeding vessel, as the mangled leg stump was prepared for surgery. Moss had to work very close to my hand to tie off the artery. Repair of the artery was not needed because there was no lower leg to be saved. So we simply sutured the artery closed to stop its bleeding.

Then we were faced with other multiple bleeding sites in the enormous open wound, and went back and forth, alternately packing the wound with gauze—to allow the anesthesiologist to catch up on blood replacement—and then to suture the various bleeding points. After an hour, Shinneman's situation changed, and we recognized that we were dealing with bleeding from new sites in his hip that had not been bleeding formerly. There was also recurrent bleeding from places we had previously controlled. His blood had lost the ability to clot. He had at that point received twenty units of blood, more than twice his normal blood volume.

The available blood on hand was bank blood and frozen blood, neither of which contained the missing factors essential for clotting. (It would take ten years before a process was developed for making available the necessary clotting factors, i.e. platelets and fresh frozen plasma, known as FFP, for just this situation.) Our only solution was to call for fresh blood from donors on base, but that process would take more than an hour.

At the same time, Shinneman's core body temperature was dropping—a sign of his worsening state—due to the extent of his wound and the loss of blood. We made a difficult choice: to ligate the femoral artery higher at the groin. This brought the risk of possibly devitalizing some of the stump tissue. By doing so, we did stop the ongoing bleeding, but had added the risk of poor wound healing due to the lack of circulation. Next, we placed a dressing on the short fat stump, with the hope that the pressure would stanch the many oozing vessels, and also help with the heat loss. Blood warmers and bed warmers were not available in Vietnam, so we used blankets that had been warmed in the autoclave. It would take time for fresh blood to arrive and the warming with blankets to work.

I stayed up in the ICU for several nights to oversee the massive fluid replacement that Shinneman needed. His body was behaving like that of a burn patient with a large area of skin loss, leaking serous fluids from the open wound. This loss of serous fluid along with his massive bleeding fortunately did not lead to irreversible multi-organ failure, yet his condition was so unstable that we needed to recalibrate his fluid-replacement needs every two hours.

Shinneman was too sick to be aware that he was close to death. But on the third night, between morphine shots and blood transfusions, he asked me in a lucid interval, "Will I die, Doc?" I knew I had to give him a thoughtful answer, not just a quick reassurance that he would be fine. I was certain he knew better than that. His situation was precarious, and the outcome unknown. I knew that an interval between morphine injections was not the time for a heart to-heart-talk, since the patient would be in and out of consciousness. So I told Shinneman the limited truth, that he had proven amazingly resilient, and that we had no intention of giving up. With that assurance, he went back to sleep.

We took him back to the OR each morning for three days, for dressing changes under anesthesia, and stitching any remaining bleeding points. But on the fourth night, after the bleeding had been controlled, his blood pressure dropped, and he had a spike in his body temperature. His heart rate quickened. The following morning, his white blood cell count was higher, and his blood pressure remained low, in spite of his having received more fluids.

When Moss arrived that fourth morning, we reviewed the situation. We both knew that Shinneman had an infected wound, despite his having received antibiotics, and would need another surgery. This would be a risky amputation through the hip joint. Moss went to confer with Adams, our most experienced surgeon, and asked me to schedule the surgery. He did not say so, but I assumed, from the unusual nature of the wound itself, that he had never done such a case. I reviewed the anatomy of the hip joint and pelvis so I could be more helpful. We went about the operation methodically, and focused so completely upon Shinneman's survival that the wish for a positive outcome for him seemed to become synonymous with our concerns for our own personal survival. His life was as important to us as our own. We sutured each intramuscular vessel with fine vascular stitches, while the anesthesia staff rotated warm blankets on the patient's torso, to ward off hypothermia.

Following this surgery, Shinneman's infection cleared, so after ten days from admission, and after receiving more than one hundred units of blood, we were able to evacuate him to Clark Air Base Hospital.

Of course, we wondered what had happened to him after his return to the United States. But except for an occasional direct encounter at Clark Air Base, when one of us had transported an unstable patient there, we rarely learned anything of our patients' fates once they had left us.

However, the day Shinneman returned to his home in South Dakota, a photo was taken of him by Ray Mews, a photographer for the Sioux Falls daily newspaper, the *Argus Leader*. In the picture, Shinneman is standing on his one leg, clutching his wife in an embrace, his crutch having fallen to the ground. The picture was syndicated and published in Sunday newspapers in August 1966, and received national attention. Relatives in the States clipped the picture from their local papers and sent them to us, not even realizing we had been personally involved. When we received those copies of the photo in the mail from home, everyone in our hospital unit glowed with pride for having saved this Marine.

Mews won many awards for the photo, and a nomination for the Pulitzer Prize. For many Americans, the picture came to symbolize their experience of Vietnam and the wish to embrace the wounded soldier who'd come home. But for us, it symbolized the unwritten story of the battlefield medicine that had allowed him—and so many others—to return to a productive and happy civilian life.

One of the fine corpsmen who was on duty with me during that time, whose name I have sadly forgotten, tracked me down thirty years later. We spoke on the phone about our having saved Shinneman. He remembered my staying with Shinneman through all those nights. In 2001, when Moss and I met for the first time since the war, we both immediately spoke of the case. The thoughtful and complicated decisions we had made in 1966 were as clear in our memories then as they had been when we had made them thirty-five years earlier.

Perry Shinneman lived a full life on one leg as a correctional officer and as a volunteer at the veteran's center in Sioux Falls. He died there at age seventy, in 2005, having survived his wife Shirley.

CHAPTER XXIII

John Wayne

Volleyball games continued much as they had during my first months at C Med. The terrain at the new Naval hospital was perfect, since the soil for the entire compound was sand (a result of its location near the South China Sea). These games were part of a routine we had, late in the day, on days when there were no heavy casualties. There were several organized teams, but usually we played pick-up matches. It was considered a serious sign of depression or fatigue if one of the regulars did not play for several days in a row. As the year ground on, I slowly began to fit such a pattern, and preferred time alone with books and letters.

My reserve of energy was nearly empty.

During the spring of 1966, after one of our games, we found the movie star John Wayne sitting with a group of doctors in the Naval hospital officer's club. Dressed in brown cowboy boots and a Stetson hat, smoking a cigarette, he chatted with the crowd around him. Just short of sixty years old, and with recent surgery for removal of a cancerous lung, he had lost some of the vitality that had made him a cultural icon. He was the star of many World War II battle movies that were often shown at Marine bases, and to us, he symbolized the ideal, good-hearted, strong American. He'd volunteered to come to Vietnam on a goodwill tour to bolster morale. His plan was to drop in on the various battalion headquarters and base camps in and around Da Nang, and to use our quarters as a home base. Wayne volunteered to make rounds with us on the post-surgical ward, to cheer up the wounded. The men he saw might have a missing leg, a big abdominal dressing with an assortment of tubes, or a head dressing with a paralyzed extremity. They all addressed him as "Sir," and were deferential to Wayne in the way they would be to a high-ranking officer.

I had found that the typical wounded Marine, during his treatment, would maintain a stunning composure well beyond his years, given his situation. On this occasion, at each bed, one of the surgeons or I would introduce the wounded man to Wayne, and describe certain medical aspects of the patient's situation. I now believe, in retrospect, that it was inappropriate to reveal such details to a layman, as a matter of patient privacy. We were unconsciously crossing that boundary because of Wayne's impressive personality and his generosity in making this protracted solo visit to men fighting an unpopular war.

In these conversations, Wayne routinely broke the ice with something like, "Where are you from, son?"

"I'm from Illinois, sir."

"No kidding. Illi...fuckin'...nois." His reply would bring a big laugh from everyone within the dimly lit Quonset hut that served as our post-op ward. "I had a girlfriend one time in Peoria, and did I get in trouble with her old man! Do you have a girlfriend, son?"

If a particular Marine did have a girlfriend, he was not going to talk about it with all these people around. These men would almost invariably deflect any concern about themselves, and almost always would express their intention to get back to their platoon. This was not a practiced or taught response. It seemed to have grown out of the experience of relying on each other for months of nearly constant patrol, in tense and terrifying situations. Only other platoon members knew how completely reshaped they all had been by the war. When they had enlisted at eighteen, they might have worried only about their looks and whether they were "cool." Now they lived or died depending on the vigilance of the men in their platoon. With their experiences, they already seemed much, much older. The family and girlfriend at home would have known and remembered quite a different young man.

John Wayne was very quiet by the time we finished rounds, and although he stayed with us another week, he never asked to see the wounded men again.

Wayne was a big supporter of the war, and two years later made the movie *The Green Berets*. He had acted in so many war films that, no doubt, part of him had assumed a real life role as a veteran. As much as we appreciated his visiting the men, he soon became for us just another civilian whose opinions about the value of the war were based on fiction. He was a legitimate celebrity and, at first, an entertaining one. But after a few days and a lot of laughter, the scene with John Wayne grew old for me. I dropped out of my routine stop at the officers' club while he was there.

Many of us had changed, from the persons we had been before the war to those we had become because of the war. Equally so, it seemed to us from what we were reading in the news and in letters from home, that the citizenry of the United States was becoming divided between those who understood the reality of war and those who did not, and between those who maintained support for this particular war and those who wanted it to end. Increasingly, the two sides were so committed to their divergent opinions that they stopped listening to each other.

All of us had made our way to Vietnam with some hope in mind: perhaps in the case of the individual Marine, that being an integral part of the *esprit de corps* would always save him. Maybe for the doctor, the unrealistic hope might be that he could save everyone who reached him alive. Possibly for everyone involved, the hope that we would restore democracy, and democracy would be Vietnam's salvation.

Then came the inevitable destruction of those hopes by the cold reality of what happens in war. I had not come close to anticipating the enormity of the horror I would witness or the emotional toll it would take on me. Few, if any, Marines seemed to realize it was possible that they, as individuals, might be seriously wounded or killed. Most of the time, I heard surprise and even disbelief when someone couldn't move an arm or a leg that was now paralyzed or mangled. Rarely would I get asked in early resuscitation in triage, "Am I going to die?" That question would come later, after that patient's surgery, as reality was sinking in. Marines who were hit in the legs or lower abdomen often asked, "Did I lose my balls?" They were not trying to be humorous, though it seemed that way to us at first. The real question, though, went unspoken: would anyone at home love them and want to be with them if they were missing body parts?

Another unexpected response from the wounded Marines was their experience of pain. The initial level of pain reported from those with major injuries was inexplicably not severe enough to elicit a request for morphine, whereas small, isolated injuries often did. The most severely injured lay quietly, their eyes closed, seemingly unaware of where they were hit, or whether a body part was missing. The standard pain score response was "ten" (on a scale of one to ten) with a broken leg, and then paradoxically decreased with the increasing severity of an injury.

Why so? The best guess is that, among the inflammatory chemicals released by the body as part of its defensive system, there are some that can quiet the mind and block the pain of massive injury. Those in shock were in the most precarious condition of all and, if they survived, they had no recall of their resuscitation or of the first day in the hospital. It was always a relief to us when their eyes and facial expressions expressed some vitality once again. When their conditions stabilized and the breathing tubes were safely removed, we would then hear their reactions: "What happened to me?" "I guess I lost my legs." "Am I going home now?"

On countless occasions, these men could have used a deeper and more personal talk with us. But the beds were two feet apart in open wards, and devoid of privacy. I was running from crisis to crisis, and not mature enough to understand the enormous emotional needs that these men no doubt had. The chaplains helped by talking to the men, though mainly these Marines bore it quietly on their own, often by making jokes about their new situations. For example, in the case of those men who had tripped mines: about who was now the shortest.

In a letter home, I reported that I was trying to bring perspective to my life and to stay healthy. I had begun running two miles a day on the road in front of the hospital at noon, sometimes in 120-degree heat. My path headed south and away from the hospital, where I could see Marble Mountain and the bunkers that formed the perimeter for the helicopter base. Sand dunes largely blocked the ocean view, but I could imagine great ocean storms flooding over this finger of land to the inland river.

Part of the reason I went running was an intense need to get away from the trauma. I had diagnosed my own depressed state once I had realized that I had met all the criteria we diagnosed in others. During the last two months of my tour, I also lost interest in getting acquainted with the newly arrived doctors. I had seen other doctors and Marines retreat into themselves, and I knew that this was a bad sign. Nightly I retreated early to my desk for reading and for going over, once again, Nancy's letters. Her letters carried her scent. They comforted me and I longed to be with her. Like Waldron before me, I had burned out. Only going home would fix my state of mind.

CHAPTER XXIV

The ARVN Civil War—Our Ally Unravels

In the same period during which we had worked on Shinneman and continued repairing other wounded men, there had been increasing unrest and bloodshed in the area. The North Vietnamese army was moving units into the I Corps region, strengthening Viet Cong forces there.

In addition, there was a major conflict in the Da Nang area among our South Vietnamese allies. The chief of the Vietnam Air Force, General Nguyen Cao Ky, a Catholic, was at odds with his major rival, the popular and flamboyant military commander of the Vietnam Army, General Nguyen Chanh Thi, who was Buddhist. In his drive for power, General Ky persuaded eight of the ten generals of the ruling junta to oust General Thi, exiling him to the U.S. in 1966.

This inflamed the long hostility that had been brewing between Catholics and Buddhists in Vietnam. All of the focus that should have been on the North Vietnamese and Viet Cong forces was now directed inward. On May 15, 1966, General Ky's South Vietnamese air force units bombed General Thi's army compound in Da Nang, hitting one of our Marine units. We received many wounded Army of the Republic of Vietnam (ARVN) soldiers, as well as U.S. troops, all of whom had been surprised and caught in the crossfire.

Because of the flood of post-op wounded, we restarted the

rapid evacuation process we had used at C Med. The dependability of the ARVN reached a new low, and many of us believed that the war was lost at that time. This specific attack—by South Vietnamese forces against South Vietnamese forces—laid bare a great weakness in the larger U.S. Vietnam plan.

One result of the bombing of General Thi's compound was that a South Vietnamese armory was left unguarded, from which American-made 105 howitzer shells were stolen by the Viet Cong. Almost immediately, we started treating many more Marines blown up by land mines that had been made from those very same shells. With this increase in the numbers of wounded, plus the news of our allies becoming unraveled, it was now impossible to ignore the fact that the war was not going well. People on all sides, military and civilians, were dying in huge numbers without any progress towards what we had believed to be the U.S. government's stated goal, of preserving and protecting the Republic of South Vietnam as a democracy.

Through all this, I just kept my head down and concentrated on the ongoing daily clinic assignments and trauma care. The most common illnesses we saw in clinic were men with amoebiasis and hookworm. There was very little malaria this season, a reversal from the previous September. The drop in malaria incidence may have been due to improved drug prophylaxis, and also because there was less rain for the mosquito-breeding cycle. We saw more acute abdominal and flank pain from renal stones, caused by dehydration. When Marines were on the move, carrying eighty pounds of equipment, they needed to drink a minimum of five canteens of liquid a day. This was difficult to achieve because reliable water sources were hard to find.

One of the calls that took me from the clinic to the OR concerned the case of a Marine who had multiple shrapnel wounds to the abdomen, producing blood in his urine, and low blood pressure. I had been doing increasingly difficult operations for nine months, but this was the first case that included severe injury to the urinary tract. Since we were not busy with other cases, I had the opportunity to be the lead surgeon on the case, under the supervision of Dr. Donald Kelly, a career Navy surgeon.

Kelly was a man with a particularly good sense of humor. He was the life of the party on those occasions when we might be having some small celebration in the officers' club. He would sometimes say that he was Cross's "opposite twin," that while Cross was a well-contained, quiet man, Kelly was the talkative one. We appreciated how, if we had had a particularly bad day, Kelly was the person to ease the distress, to lighten it.

On this occasion, we X-rayed the patient's abdomen, to estimate what organs had been hit and to assure ourselves that shrapnel had not also penetrated his chest. Most abdominal cases were exploratory surgeries, because the extent of injury could not be known until the abdomen was opened. This case required urgent control of a bleeding vessel, with stitches being placed near a rapidly forming pool of blood.

Kelly's experience was evident as he controlled both sides of the bleeding mesentery, thus making my job easier. As we worked, he talked about the skill required to be a good assistant in surgery, to anticipate what the surgeon needs. My mind drifted back to my own internship, and I remembered a resident surgeon joking, "If I could just assist myself, I could be the best surgeon in the world."

That concept may have been the reason Kelly had me operating with him as assistant. He knew the value of good interactive teaching, and how surgical training could be enhanced by sometimes giving an assistant a more major role in a surgical procedure.

I used that lesson many times later in life, in my own training of surgical residents. There were many occasions during which I could expedite their learning if I assisted them, rather than having them assist me. Often this has ultimately resulted in a better outcome for the patient.

After controlling this particular patient's bleeding, and letting the anesthesiologist catch up with blood replacement, we started checking closely the six feet of his colon and the longer small bowel, where we found many shrapnel holes. We removed two feet of damaged colon, and brought the open ends of the colon to the surface as colostomies. The wounds to the small bowel, which has better blood supply and fewer bacteria than other areas of the body, were debrided and closed. We also debrided the bladder wound, and inserted a Foley catheter to keep the bladder emptied, to avoid straining the suture line. We always scrutinized the entire abdomen before closing, since a missed injury would cause peritonitis, an infection in the abdomen that could be fatal.

I followed my patient long enough to see him eating and well into recovery, before he left with what we called a "million-dollar wound" (alive, but injured enough to return to the United States). It is true that the identities of most of the Marines on which we operated were lost to us surgeons. There were simply too many patients, and we didn't have time to enquire about who they actually were. However, years after the Vietnam War, my 14 year-old daughter was attending a summer camp, when one of the directors asked her if her father had been a doctor in Da Nang in 1966, at a time when he, a Marine then, had been seriously wounded. When the fact of my service there was confirmed, he explained that my daughter's name "Trueblood" was so distinctive in his memory of Vietnam that that was the reason for his question. Perhaps this was the very man whose identity was lost in the chaos of the numbers of wounded bodies.

As for our own return home, each of us had arrived in Vietnam one by one, and now we were leaving one by one, with no debriefings or preparation for reentering what had become almost a forgotten world.

CHAPTER XXV

Naval Hospital, July 1966

"Communist mortar men rained 30 shells tonight..."
—Robert Tuckman, (AP), Saigon, July 21, 1966

Pitlyk and I were standing over a patient one night in the intensive care unit when we heard the familiar *whump whump whump* firings of far-away mortars, then a pause, then the sound of three explosions in the nearly empty adjacent ward. After we doused the lights, we ran out the back door and jumped into a foxhole. There was a second round of shelling that marched across the road and hit the MAG 16 helicopter base. A total of thirty shells dropped on or near our hospital that night.

A mortar firing sequence contains two sounds, ironically, just as there are two sounds to a heartbeat: lub-dub, lub-dub. You hear the first as the mortar is being fired, and the second sound when it lands and explodes. The firing sound is a flat one, while the landing and exploding sound is loud and sharply definitive. The silent pause between the two sounds spans the arching flight of the shell.

Lying on the ground, in the foxhole, listening to the ominous sequence, I held the sickening knowledge that at that moment, someone was trying to kill me. Having been shelled the previous year during Harvest Moon, I now knew that each subsequent experience became more, rather than less, frightening. I had a more complete understanding of the effect of shrapnel on the body, and had seen the size of the craters in the ground. In my early days in Da Nang, I had thought that I eventually would toughen myself against the physical threat implicit in each attack. Instead, just one month from going home, this particular attack left me quite shaken. Knowing, as I had learned, that this form of attack was often a suicide mission on the part of the Viet Cong did little to calm my nerves.

The Marines guarding our compound were able to locate the origin of the attack, and counter-attacked. Within an hour, our lights went back on. We quickly assessed our damages—fifteen minor casualties—and were back in business.

Luckily, no one died that night.

After everything was under control and I went back to my tent, I reread an earlier letter from home. My father wrote that he'd picked out the new red Volvo 122 I'd asked him to buy with money I'd saved from combat duty. The car cost $2,800 out of my $8,000 pay for the year. This was a joint decision with Nancy. "Dad tells me the Volvo is in the driveway," I wrote to Nancy. "It will take us to our wedding."

The anticipation of that day, and of Nancy and me in that car, provided the spark of enthusiasm I needed to endure. The car in the driveway seemed like a promise I would return to a normal life. I was getting closer to the end of my time in Vietnam. Thirty days and counting. Like the Marines in the field, I was acutely aware of the amount of time left, and like them, I counted down the days. Every day.

CHAPTER XXVI

Homeward Bound

For the last several months in Vietnam, I had a day job running a General Medical Clinic that saw up to forty military patients each day. There were more than fifty thousand Navy and Marine personnel in our region. The illness list was full of cases of diarrhea, malaria, bites, cuts, broken bones, alcohol intoxication, appendicitis, hernias, venereal disease, psychiatric problems, and self-inflicted injuries. The corpsmen at the clinic were so skilled that they rarely needed me there. Of course, given the major casualties we were seeing, these cases seemed trivial, but I was happy for the respite. Later, when my children were growing up, they were to kid me that I never took their illnesses seriously unless bleeding was involved.

As my last months in Vietnam ground on, I developed the well-known paranoia called "short-timers syndrome." I felt increasingly vulnerable to the possibility of fluky accidents, and actually feared that a major offensive would cancel all departures. In this state of mind, I reduced my life to a routine of essentials, trying to become invisible.

I was temporarily brought out of this state on the day that word spread throughout the base that we had a patient with a live mortar shell in his chest.

There were two such cases in the span of a few months at

the Naval hospital, and both were managed by the most senior surgeons at the time. The first by Adams and the other by Dr. Harry Dinsmore, who had come in as our new chief of surgery. For safety reasons, we were all excluded from both events.

Really, this is Dinsmore's story. As he recalls it, on arrival the patient, a 108-pound Vietnamese solider, was surprisingly calm, with a normal blood pressure, with only slightly rapid breathing. X-ray suggested that neither the chest cavity nor the abdominal cavities had been entered; rather, the mortar had penetrated the skin just below the clavicle and then plowed a hole between ribs and muscle. The mortar was identified as a Soviet 60 mm, with the fuse only partially depressed. On its descent the shell had hit a glancing blow to the roof of a truck, and then a soldier's helmet, causing it to lose speed before land-ing. The shell did not detonate because of the gradual loss of velocity and its ultimate landing in the soft tissue of the chest of the wounded solider. This had prevented the full depression of the fuse.

The patient was moved from triage to the open walkway between X-ray and surgery, while Dinsmore sought advice from the ordinance man, a Marine whose name was Lyons. Dinsmore was told that under no circumstance should he twist or pull the shell. Were he to do so, Lyons pointed out, the action might activate the fuse.

The entire area was made off limits to everyone except Din-smore, Lyons, the attending anesthesiologist and one assisting corpsman. Inside the OR, sand bags were placed around the operating table, except for a space for the surgeon to stand on the patient's left. Dinsmore himself could not be protected by more than a flak jacket. The sand bags would limit damage to the OR if detonation occurred.

The patient was given heavy sedation by the anesthesiolo-gist, who then went to the next room, beyond the sandbags, with Lyons and the surgical corpsman. The three men waited, hoping not to be called back to Dinsmore's lonely task.

The surgery began when Dinsmore cut a long ellipse around the bulging chest mass, sacrificing skin and soft tissue, with the goal of lifting the mortar out without tension. He struggled when he encountered the man's shirt, still attached to itself at the sleeve, deep in the wound. The detail of the shirt had been forgotten because of the necessary decision (given the presence of the live shell in the man's body) not to prep the surgical site. After cutting the shirt free, Dinsmore was able to very delicately extract the missile itself. Holding it in his hands, he called to Lyons, to whom he handed it off, together with the surrounding soft tissue, skin, and the compacted shirt, all in one piece. Lyons took the missile—with extreme care—to a nearby sand dune, where he deactivated the fuse.

Recalling the event later, Dinsmore said, "I embarked upon the longest thirty minutes of my life." A more detailed account is given in Jan K. Herman's 2010 book *Navy Medicine in Vietnam*. In 1966, there was also a *Life* magazine article about the event, in which the reader can see the Vietnamese patient in bandages, recovering from surgery. In another photo, Dinsmore holds the defused mortar shell in one hand. It is a foot long, several inches wide, and shaped like a 1950s-era toy rocket-ship.

Dinsmore's bravery, and that of the many other surgeons who did similar extractions, ranks with the highest order of heroic actions known in warfare. This was not a spontaneous act on Dinsmore's part. He had plenty of time beforehand to think over the consequences, a realization that makes the calm with which he undertook the surgery that day even more extraordinary. Dr. Harry Dinsmore was awarded the Navy Cross for his heroic action.

CHAPTER XXVII

So Sorry, Vietnam

One evening in mid-August, just days before my scheduled return to the United States, a medevac helicopter arrived with three wounded Marines and a Vietnamese mother holding a small baby girl. The baby was breathing rapidly and her skin had a blue pallor. Since the wounds of the Marine casualties weren't severe, I turned my attention to the sick baby. The way she was breathing, and her color, made me think of a congenital heart defect situation that I had seen as an intern, on the heart surgery service at HUP. Listening to the little girl's chest with my stethoscope revealed the telltale systolic murmur of such an affliction. I knew that, in Vietnam at that time, no Vietnamese surgeons were doing repairs for this problem, and that the American heart surgeons had neither the vital heart-lung machine so essential to such an undertaking, nor the team to perform the surgery itself.

I chose to intervene and treat the baby with digitalis, a drug used to strengthen a failing heart. I was still at the stage of my career in which I was sure that there was an intervention for every problem. I wanted to show the Vietnamese mother that Americans could fix, not just destroy. I calculated a proper dose of digitalis several times, based on the little girl's body weight, and then I gave her the drug.

She died within minutes.

I was stunned. I had unintentionally precipitated the girl's death, and all I could do was hand back her lifeless body to her mother. Having no words for her in Vietnamese, I simply said, "So sorry, so sorry." The mother did not cry, but merely turned and walked away, carrying her dead baby into the night.

If I had thought this through in advance, I would have decided that there was nothing anyone could do for this baby in this war-wrecked country. The little girl had come to us barely alive, and any drug would simply have been a temporizing measure. Her heart had been racing out of internal necessity, due to the hole between its chambers. The digitalis, although strengthening the heart muscle, slowed the heart rate enough so that delivery of oxygen to the brain was diminished.

I felt absolutely horrible. I had never been so directly responsible for ending a patient's life with an intervention that I had supervised. I sat down with my head in my hands, literally reeling.

I lay awake a long time that night trying to rationalize my action, and worrying about the mother. Was she blaming herself as parents do? I had seen that the baby was malnourished, and now could not imagine how the little girl had been able to nurse while so short of breath. I thought that the mother had shown great courage to have asked a Marine in her little village for help, and then had been willing to get on the helicopter by herself, sheltering her sick little baby, with foreign soldiers whom she could not understand. I also thought a lot about her lack of tears.

Several minutes after she had left the hospital, I realized that she might not know the way to her distant village. Who would befriend and help a lost woman with a dead baby on the outskirts of Da Nang? Would she find her way home?

I had other patients. I couldn't run outside and try to find her, to try to help her.

I'm still haunted by the memory of that woman and her

baby. The mother was left with a crushing loss, and I had been an active participant in her child's inevitable death. It is clear to me that, in the moment of the decision that I made that day, I had not yet gained the wisdom of knowing when not to intervene.

Over the course of my year there, I had gradually begun to realize that our military intervention in Vietnam was not going at all well. In addition to the number of wounded men in triage and in the OR, which was increasing every day, we noted that very few of these men had actually seen enemy soldiers. Also, we realized that the wounded and killed Marines that we encountered had been injured in actions that had taken place in the same general territory, in the same manner, time and again. The most common pattern of injury was on patrol, when the lead man of an infantry squad would trip a booby-trap shell that had been placed during the night by the Viet Cong. His legs would be blown off, and five or six other members of the platoon would suffer multiple shrapnel wounds from the same explosion. A Viet Cong sniper would then pin down the squad and shoot the corpsman coming to the aid of the wounded.

One can imagine the demoralization we regularly felt when we would see yet another helicopter-load of body bags and injured men coming from the same places from which the helicopters had come with previous bags, and with men injured in the same way, all of their wounds telling the same tale.

We had very little sense of the actual enemy, except for the fact that we knew they had been in this war for a long time, and were not going home after a one-year tour. They were organized and committed, and knew this terrain. Eventually, most of the doctors, chaplains and corpsmen that I knew came to the same conclusion, through talking with the wounded, visiting with Recon men or the always-informed Seabees: that the war seemed ill-conceived.

In spite of our discouragement, we had a job to do: to attend to our wounded Marines. And that's what we did.

On August 23, 1966, at Da Nang airbase, wearing stained fatigues and boots, I boarded a C130 for the flight to Clark Air Force Base, and then to Okinawa. We banked east, and I got my last view of the green jungle-covered mountains—so beautiful, deadly, and blood-drenched. I slept through the layover at Clark, and woke up in Okinawa at the air base.

There I went to the men's room, undressed, threw my boots and fatigues in the trash, and put on the dress khakis that I had worn only twice before: once when I had shipped out to Vietnam a year ago, the second time on R&R in Bangkok. I now weighed 140 pounds, down twenty from when I had arrived. From Travis Air Force Base in Fairfield, California, I got a ride on a West Virginian Air National Guard plane to Chicago. I slept through one of my connecting flights from Chicago to Des Moines, but I was able to phone Nancy in Syracuse, at her parents' home where she had moved in the past month, to prepare for our wedding. I was overjoyed to hear her voice. We planned for her to travel to Iowa, where she would meet my parents for the first time.

My parents greeted me at the airport. They had noticeably aged that year. Mom had endured Dad's being away for three years during World War II. Having a son in war had been terribly hard on her. When I got home to Indianola, the new red Volvo was in the driveway. I went directly through the house to the back yard, where, as a child, I had played with my sisters and neighbors, and our dogs. I fell to the grass and sobbed amidst the flowers, the trees and the sweet, dark soil of home.

Nancy flew to Iowa two days later. As I waited for her in the Des Moines airport, observing the other people waiting, I saw no sense, in their faces or demeanor, that they knew young

American men were being shot and blown up in a foreign land twelve thousand miles away. I was enraged by these people. In that moment, I thought that surely every day should be a national day of mourning. Not one of them had any idea of what the men I had treated had been through

I had to brush the notion aside, though. I was here to meet Nancy. I was rattled with nerves. Sweat ran down my arms. What if I did not recognize her, or she me? Would I still love this person whom I had loved this past year only through the exchange of our letters?

The plane was unloading at a very slow pace. Finally she appeared, the last down the ramp, wearing a blue summer suit. Of course we recognized each other instantaneously. Her eyes lit up the moment she saw me. She must have shared some of my worries, giving me a reserved, yet nonetheless warm smile. All my lingering thoughts were erased simply by the act of holding her in my arms. I did not want to stop holding her, but I also wanted to feast my eyes on her at arm's length. Words were not necessary. They have never been essential for us when we are together.

My memory of that moment of loving embrace with Nancy in the Des Moines airport would provide me with the impetus to neglect the memory of what I had seen and lived in Vietnam. Decades later, though, it would also be pivotal in allowing me finally to contemplate the year I spent there—which was both the worst and the most defining year of my life.

Nancy and I were married at the Most Holy Rosary church in Syracuse, New York. I was dressed for the first time in my life in a morning suit, with all the usual accouterments. Many of my relatives (aunts, uncles and cousins) traveled from Pennsylvania and Iowa to Syracuse, and made of the journey a two-part celebration: in part they wanted to acknowledge my safe return home from Vietnam. Just as much, of course, they wanted to meet the person I had decided to marry. Several of my friends from Earlham College and my internship time at Penn were also there. While I had made close friendships in Vietnam, many of them were still engaged in the service and not able to join us. Of my Stanford classmates, half of them too were still serving in Vietnam.

The night before our wedding, my brothers-in-law David Kem and Richard Blum gathered the men together for the bachelor party, which we held in my hotel room. There were many funny stories, along with many questions for me about Vietnam. I deflected those. I had been home a mere two weeks, and it was too soon for me to have thoughtful opinions about what I had seen and done there.

I had gotten through the ordeal simply by dealing with each day at a time. For years I was to deal with my return to civilian life similarly until, to be sure, Vietnam revisited me—was forced upon me—many years later in the form of increased personal irritability and vivid dreams.

I did not sleep well the night before our wedding. That was not due to any doubt about my decision; rather I was beginning to understand the magnitude of this step I was taking, not just for a year, but for the rest of my life. Also, in these early days of my return home, I was like every other returning veteran that I knew, knowing at some profound level of the critical need to return more fully to ordinary life, regardless of what my experience of war had been. I did not make an intentional decision to put aside the memory of the past year, But some voice—most probably of personal sanity—caused me to do it. I suspect that all those who were able to return successfully had somehow to find a similar path, even though we all likely have continued to carry our own emotional wounds.

The wedding was a joyous celebration of love, and now man and wife, Nancy and I drove from the church in the red Volvo.

Rather than off into the sunset, a few days later the Volvo

took us to the Naval hospital in Jacksonville, Florida, where I would serve out the second year of my commitment to the U.S. Navy. The car would become like a part of the family, holding as many memories as any inanimate object can. A year after our wedding, it carried us across the country to Stanford University, where I would finish my surgical training. Eventually, it became the learning-to-drive car for both our children, and, to be sure, suffered a few traumas from the treatment it got during those years. As the car passed through year after year, I begun having actual nightmares of its stalling on a hill, unable to keep moving at all, the victim, finally, of old age.

But I still was unwilling to sell the car. The notion, during the last month of my service in Vietnam, of its waiting for me in the driveway of my parents' home—of my returning home alive, of marrying Nancy, the chance to lead a normal life in America, to have children, happiness, and safety—had been one to which I had clung. So when the Volvo was 25 years old, Nancy and I gave the car to her brother Tom, who lives in Tucson, Arizona. Giving up the car entirely, and the memories it has for us, was something I simply would not do. It remains with our family. Tom thought that restoring it would be a good joint project with his teenage son. I now picture the red Volvo, almost good as new, resting in the desert weather at Tom's house.

CHAPTER XXVIII

Home

The extent of the experience I had gained in Vietnam came to the fore when I returned to civilian life in 1967, to complete my surgical residency at Stanford. On one of my first nights on call, we received a patient with a gunshot wound to the abdomen. I was the senior surgical resident in the hospital. The young man was in shock, and the bullet had entered his abdominal right upper quadrant. The X-ray localized the bullet near the second lumbar vertebra. We placed a call to our supervising physician, Dr. Robert Mason, to alert him to the case.

It was unheard of for a resident to take a case to the OR without an attending physician present. Dr. Mason nonetheless convinced the OR nurses of the urgent need to proceed while he was en route to the hospital.

We found holes in the patient's gall bladder, his duodenum, and a hematoma around his vena cava that indicated that fatal bleeding could occur at any time. I kept looking through the OR window for Dr. Mason, but continued on.

I moved the duodenum and the right colon to the midline, and exposed the vena cava. I then directed the intern to occlude the one-inch wide vein above and below the front entrance hole, by compressing the vena cava against the vertebra while I sutured it. We then rolled the vena cava over, and repaired the exit hole the same way.

By the time Dr. Mason arrived in the OR, the bleeding had been controlled. We discussed with him how to proceed with the duodenal repair, and as he left, with me still in charge, he looked back over his shoulder and said, "Nice work."

POSTSCRIPT

Life After 1967

Nancy Young married Ward Trueblood two weeks after his return from Vietnam. They had two children, Hope and Nathan. Nancy eventually made a professional transition from nursing to psychology, earning a master's degree in psychology and counseling. Nancy and both children all received advanced degrees during the same weekend. Nancy continues her private practice of psychotherapy on the peninsula south of San Francisco.

Dr. Bruce Canaga was assigned, after his service in Vietnam, to The United States Naval Academy as chief medical officer. After his navy career, he entered private practice in Portsmouth, Virginia. He died in 1987.

Dr. Greg Cross returned from Vietnam to the San Diego Naval Hospital, and later became chairman of the Department of Surgery at Great Lakes Naval Hospital. He then assumed the same position at Portsmouth Naval Hospital. After retirement from the Navy, he became medical director of a major civilian hospital in Portsmouth, Virginia. He is now retired.

Dr. Harry Dinsmore was chief of surgery at the Naval Support Activity Hospital in Da Nang. He was awarded the Navy Cross for service and valor above and beyond the call of duty. He was also awarded the Victory Medal (World War II), the Republic of Vietnam Medal and the Vietnamese Cross of

Gallantry with Silver Star, which was the highest Vietnamese award. In 1967, Dr. Dinsmore opened a private practice in Punxsutawney, Pennsylvania, from which he retired in 1991. He died in 2003.

Dr. Ben Eiseman served in World War II, Korea, Viet Nam, and in various U.S. Navy medical capacities during Operation Desert Storm in 1990. He retired from the Navy Reserves as a Rear Admiral in 1974. Between stints in the U.S. Navy, he enjoyed a career in Denver, Colorado, beginning at the Denver Veterans Administration Medical Center as chief of surgery in 1953. He was then recruited to become the first chief of surgery at the College of Medicine at the University of Kentucky. He returned to Denver in 1967, to assume the position of chief of surgery at the then Denver General Hospital. He died in 2012.

Dr. Richard Escajeda, after his time in Vietnam, became Chief of Surgery at the U.S. Naval Hospital at Camp Pendleton. Once leaving the Navy, he entered the practice of plastic and reconstructive surgery in the San Diego area, where he still lives.

Dr. Donald Kelly was assigned after Vietnam to the staff of San Diego Naval Hospital, where he joined Dr. Greg Cross. After his time in the Navy, he returned to New England and private practice. He died in 2003.

Dr. Gerald Moss was chairman of the Surgery Department, and later Dean of the University of Illinois at Chicago College of Medicine. On active duty in Vietnam, he ran the Navy's trauma research project in that country, and was officer in charge of the Frozen Blood Program in Da Nang. He now lives in Florida, but remains active professionally in Chicago.

Dr. William Clarence Adams, a career Navy officer, returned to the San Diego Naval Hospital after his time in Vietnam. He later lived in Oceanside, California, and died at the age of 92 in 2014.

Dr. Paul Pitlyk remained in the Navy Reserves while enjoying a long career in the private practice of neurosurgery on the San Francisco peninsula. He is now retired. His work in Vietnam helped to revolutionize wartime neurosurgery by decreasing the urgency of removing all foreign bodies from the undamaged brain. He is the author of *Blood On China Beach*, a memoir of his time in Vietnam.

Dr. Richard Lloyd Waldron returned to Tyler, Texas. In 1966, he founded a private practice in anesthesiology in Tyler. In 1968, he was presented with the Navy Commendation Medal, in recognition of meritorious service. After retiring from private practice, Dr. Waldron helped form the Trauma Center at East Texas Medical Center. He died in 2012.

Dr. Almon Wilson served as an officer with the U.S. Navy in World War II, after which he returned to civilian life. In 1965-66, he was commanding officer of the Third Medical Battalion in Da Nang, Vietnam. After attending the Naval War College, he was medical officer on the staff of Commander in Chief, Naval Forces Europe. Dr. Wilson is known as the father of the Naval Fleet Hospital Program. The design and construction of the fleet hospitals that evolved under his guidance have transformed naval medicine. In 1991, following the Persian Gulf War, he was officially commended by the Secretary of the Navy for the performance of those hospitals. During his career, he also served as personal physician to the chairman of the Joint Chiefs of Staff, and became the first medical flag officer assigned to the U.S. Marine Corps headquarters. He retired from the Navy with the rank of Rear Admiral. He died in 2003.

Lewis W. Walt was named Assistant Commandant of the U.S Marine Corps on January 1, 1968, his last command. Beloved by the Marines in the field, he had achieved the rank of four-star general. He died in 1989. His obituary in the *New York Times* described him as "a tireless advocate of what he called 'the other war' in Vietnam: winning the hearts and minds of Vietnamese civilians. One year the Marines under his command distributed 2.5 million pounds of food and 237,000 pounds of clothing, and built 673 houses and 159 classrooms."

GLOSSARY OF TERMS

AK 47: Also known as a Kalashnikov, the AK 47 is a semi-automatic and automatic assault rifle that was developed in the Soviet Union. In the Vietnam War, it was the weapon of choice of North Vietnamese and Viet Cong ground forces.

ARVN: The Army of The Republic of Vietnam. The South Vietnamese army that fought as an ally of the United States forces.

Bird Colonel: The most senior field grade military officer rank, immediately above that of a lieutenant colonel and just below brigadier general. The term "bird colonel" is derived from the eagle insignia on the officer's uniform.

C Med: One of the many U.S. Navy field hospitals (which are similar to a Mobile Army Surgical Hospital, or MASH), serving Marines in the Vietnam War.

C-130: A large military aircraft used to transport significant numbers of Marines as well as cargo.

Commander: The first senior commissioned officer rank in the U.S. Navy, and the equivalent to the rank of lieutenant colonel in the other U.S. armed forces.

Da Nang, South Vietnam: A major city in Vietnam that is located on the coast of the South China Sea. Located in what was I Corps (see below) during the Vietnam War, Da Nang was a major center for American military activity in that theater of operations. C Med and the Naval hospital, both prominent in this account, were located in Da Nang.

DOA: Short for "dead on arrival."

Free-Fire Zone: In Vietnam, this was any area from which forces friendly to American and South Vietnamese military had officially been cleared. Under such conditions, anyone unidentified within the area would be considered an enemy combatant. Friendly forces were authorized to shoot anyone moving around the free-fire zone after curfew, without first having to make sure that that person was hostile.

Graves Registration: A Marine unit tasked with the identification of Marines killed in battle. Graves Registration was also charged with notifying next of kin in the case of a Marine's death.

Ho Chi Minh: A Vietnamese Communist revolutionary leader who was prime minister from 1945 to 1955 and president of North Vietnam from 1945 to 1969. Ho was a key figure in the foundation of the People's Army of Vietnam and, during the Vietnam War, the Viet Cong. (See below.) He led the nation of North Vietnam throughout most of the Vietnam War. He officially stepped down from power in 1965 due to health problems, but remained a highly visible figurehead until his death in 1969. "Ho Chi Minhs" was also the name given to the ubiquitous black plastic sandals worn by Ward Trueblood and other medical personnel during their time in Vietnam.

I Corps: In The Vietnam War, the First Corps Tactical Zone consisted of the five northernmost provinces of South Vietnam: Quang Tri, Thua Thien, Quang Nam, Quang Tin, and Quang Ngai. I Corps, where half the combat deaths in the Vietnam War took place, bordered Laos and North Vietnam. Da Nang is located in what was I Corps.

MAG 16: The 3rd Marine Aircraft Wing – Group 16. A U.S. Marine aviation group whose mission is to provide combat-ready expeditionary forces by air, on short notice. In Vietnam, MAG 16's most well-known duty was to bring combat-ready Marines to the drop-sites from which, on foot, the Marines would then seek out and engage any enemy forces. MAG 16 also evacuated Marines when necessary and brought wounded Marines to locations like C Med for medical care.

Seabees: A Seabee is a member of the U.S. Naval Construction Forces (NCF). The word "Seabee" comes from the initials "CB," which in turn come from the term "Construction Battalions." In Vietnam, the Seabees were in charge of building the Naval hospital in Da Nang, among many other projects.

Triage: The process of determining the priority of patients' treatments based on the severity of their condition. At C Med in Vietnam, the severity of wounds suffered by Marines was determined in the triage tent, prior to any Marines being moved into the operating room for surgery.

USOM: The United States Overseas Mission, a hospital set up in Da Nang during the Vietnam War, in which South Vietnamese citizens were treated.

Viet Cong: The name given by Western sources to the National Liberation Front, a political organization with its own army in South Vietnam and Cambodia, which fought against the United States and South Vietnamese governments during the war in Vietnam. The Viet Cong had both guerrilla and regular army units, as well as a network of cadres who organized peasants in the territory it controlled.

The Vietnam Peoples Army: The formal army of the North Vietnamese government during the Vietnam War.

105 Howitzer: The 105mm Howitzer M3 is a light cannon designed for use by airborne troops. Originally used by United States forces in World War II, it was also an important weapon in the Vietnam War.

ABOUT THE AUTHOR

Henry Ward Trueblood M.D. grew up in Indianola, Iowa, where his father was the town doctor. By the age of ten he was regularly making house calls with his father. He graduated from Earlham College in Richmond, Indiana, and went on to Stanford Medical School, where he received AOA honors, and graduated in 1964. In his second year of surgical training at the University of Pennsylvania he was drafted by the U.S. Navy. Trueblood was assigned to the first Marine Corps hospital, known as C Med, in Da Nang, Vietnam and later to the Naval Hospital on China Beach in Da Nang.

After the war, Trueblood completed his surgical training at Stanford. He currently serves as Trauma Attending at Santa Clara Valley Medical Center, a Level One Trauma Center, where he also teaches bedside skills to third-year Stanford medical students. Trueblood is the recipient of the Henry J. Kaiser Family Foundation Award for Excellence in Clinical Teaching, Stanford University School of Medicine, and the John Austin Collins Memorial Award presented by Stanford Surgical House Staff to the Outstanding Facility Teacher. In 2010, he was named an Alumnus of The Year from Earlham College.

He is the author of a book of poetry, *To Bind Up Their Wounds*, published in 2008, and a member of the Pegasus Physicians Writers Group at Stanford.

Dr. Trueblood's wife Nancy is in private practice as a psychotherapist on the San Francisco Peninsula. They have two children and five grandchildren.

If you enjoyed this book, please consider reviewing it,
and find more titles by Astor & Lenox
at http://astorandlenox.com.

Made in the USA
San Bernardino, CA
20 November 2015